The Gift of an Elephant

A story about Life, Love and Africa

JACQUIE GAUTHIER

First published in 2015

Copyright © 2015 Jacquie Gauthier

Edited by Tracey Hawthorne

Cover, maps and artwork by Sarah Currie

CreateSpace Independent Publishing Platform

ISBN 1515399079

To my family and friends, especially Mom and Dad,
who love, encourage and support me, no matter what.
And there's been a lot of "what".

To Grandma Lena and her beloved Mr Gordon,
who proved it's never too late to find the love of your life.

To my wonderful husband Johann – I choose you again today.

And to anyone who's feeling stuck in their life, particularly at a
certain age, when it feels like it's too late to change, too late to
risk, or that this is as good as it gets –
I want to tell you it's not over.
If you can hear the call of something more and can take the
leap of faith, your life can change
in ways you never could have imagined.

Acknowledgments

This story is a snapshot of my thoughts, feelings and experiences as a proverbial "stranger in a strange land". I'm eternally grateful to all the amazing South Africans who have taken me into their hearts and their homes, and who have shared their stories with me. We each view the world through a unique lens that has been shaped by our circumstances and our experiences. It is with great respect and without judgment that I relate some of these stories here.

I particularly want to thank Franz and Thelma Kleynhans – I wouldn't have made it through the first month without you.

I'll always be grateful to Don and Nina Scott for allowing me to have the experience of a lifetime at Tanda Tula. And to the staff members of Tanda Tula, all I can say is that I've been deeply privileged to have been part of your very special family.

I owe a great deal of thanks to my dear friends Lena Zwicker, Sarah Currie and Anthony Partipilo, for their support in reading the first draft of this work. Because of their feedback, I found the courage to carry on.

I am so grateful for the friendship and support of Tracy den Dunnen, Lynn Davis and Marita Albrecht. Thank you for believing in me.

Thanks to Carolyn Wilker and Susan Delacourt for their insights and suggestions early on in the project, and to my friend Frances Sullivan for her wisdom, her talents and most of all for helping me across the finish line.

Thank you, Tracey Hawthorne, for your astute observations, suggestions and editing expertise. And Sarah Currie, thanks for the gorgeous cover design and for being wonderful you!

I'm extremely grateful for the guidance of the amazing Tony Park, who was so very generous and gracious in sharing his time and advice even as he was under great pressure to finish a manuscript of his own. You're one in a million, Tony!

Foreword

I first met Jacquie Gauthier by the swimming pool at the luxurious Tanda Tula tented safari camp in South Africa's Timbavati Private Game Reserve.

I was living it up as a guest of the owners, but Jacquie was hard at work, conducting advanced English literacy classes for the camp's African rangers and hospitality staff. Her love for Africa and the continent's people was obvious from the moment I met her.

Like many people I meet in the course of my life as an author, Jacquie told me she wanted to write a book – in fact, she was well into her manuscript. Unlike many of those people, Jacquie actually finished her story.

As a rule, I'm reluctant to read other people's written works – I'm not a publisher or an editor, and don't pretend to know what deserves to be published and what doesn't. However, from what I already knew of Jacquie and her life story, I knew I would at least be interested in the subject matter.

The Gift of an Elephant hooked me from the beginning. It's a story as beautiful and moving as it is simple. Girl meets boy, girl falls in love with boy, and they move to his home country.

But this is Africa and nothing goes according to plan. Jacquie's tale of love and romance moves from war-ravaged Sudan to her native Canada, and to the stunning wildlife-rich South African bush.

This is as much a story of a love affair with a continent as it is a relationship between two people. Africa is as troubled as it is beautiful, as harsh as it is bountiful, and as challenging as it is liberating.

Jacquie captures the essence of what it's like to live in modern Africa, and what it's like trying to negotiate the often rocky, sometimes sad, but nonetheless enjoyable, heart-warming and funny journey that is her life.

Tony Park

Author: *Silent Predator*, *The Prey*, *The Hunter*

"Sometimes good things fall apart
so better things can fall together."

– *Marilyn Monroe*

"You miss 100% of the shots you don't take."

– *Wayne Gretzky*

"Change is hard."

– *Billy Crystal*

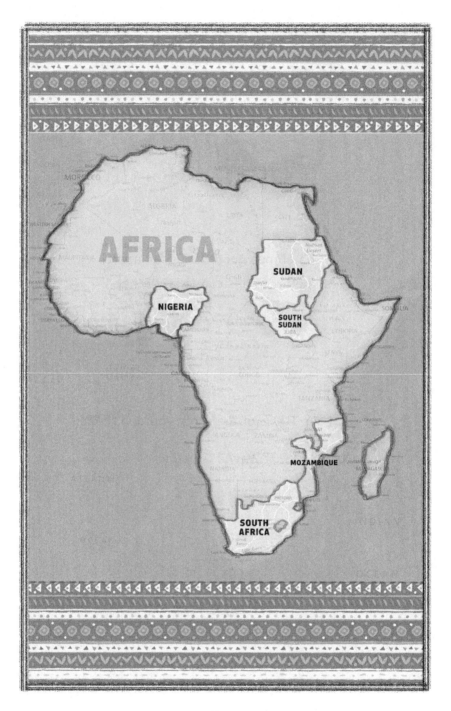

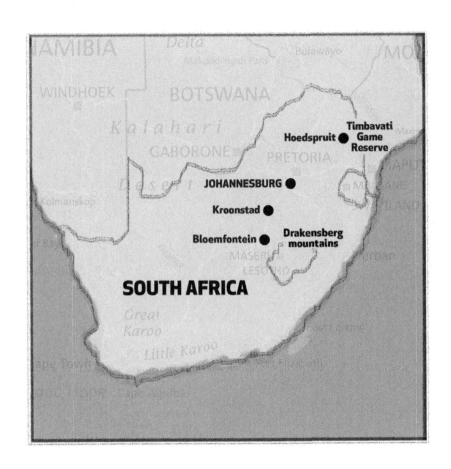

1

Limpopo province, South Africa

February 2012

My husband just left me.

Mere moments ago I stood sobbing in the scorching sun as I watched him and the little silver rental car disappear down the dirt driveway and turn onto the potholed tar road. In about five hours, he'll be at Johannesburg airport. From there, he'll board a small plane headed for Mozambique.

I should probably mention he is coming back, but not for thirty days, and at this moment it's hard to tell the difference between one month and forever.

Now, with the little silver car long gone, I'm forced to admit that staring down that desolate road will do nothing to bring it back or make the time go by any faster. I turn and slowly walk up the driveway to the back of the property and enter the little brick cottage that is now my home.

I'm dreading this month apart. I'm normally a very independent and self-sufficient person, and I am pretty good company if I do say so myself, but I'm still trying to find my footing here.

When I left Canada just a few weeks ago to move to my husband's home country, it was the dead of winter and the temperature had plummeted to minus 40 degrees Celsius. After a 26-hour journey, I found myself in the middle of a South African summer with temperatures hovering around plus 40 degrees Celsius. An 80-degree temperature swing in just over a day is definitely a shock to the system.

The radical change in the weather I'm experiencing is a pretty good indicator of how different everything else is here, too.

My husband Johann was born in Pretoria and grew up in Bloemfontein, both big cities. We've chosen to live in a small rural area not too far from the Mozambican border, so it's a big adjustment for him, too.

We arrived in this part of South Africa a few weeks ago so we could get to meet some people and familiarise ourselves with our new surroundings before he had to leave me to go back to his new job – a one-month-on/one-month-off position as a paramedic running a medical clinic in northern Mozambique. Knowing I'd be spending so much time on my own, it was critical that we picked the right place as a home base. We can already tell that we've chosen well, even without the benefit of realizing that we'd been here once before.

Two weeks ago, as we were making our way along the winding two-lane highway heading north from Johannesburg, the stunning scenery suddenly seemed familiar. It turned out we got married not far from here. In the haste and excitement of our elopement, neither of us had consulted a map. Johann had simply followed the directions he'd found on the website, and because we didn't actually drive through the small town of Hoedspruit, we were not familiar with the name.

It was a great place for a wedding, and I'm sure it will be a wonderful place to live. The people here are friendly and welcoming. This is a tight-knit community where everyone knows their neighbours. The crime rate is low, and that's no small consideration when choosing a place to live in South Africa. There are no bars on the windows here, and we don't have to live behind locked gates. It doesn't get better than that. At least Johann doesn't have to worry about my safety while he's away; just my sanity.

Before I go any further, I should tell you what I now understand is an important fact about my husband. He's a white South African. When I first told my parents about this lovely South African man I'd met, it didn't occur to me to mention his race. When I showed them my only photo of Johann and me, there was an awkward silence before my mom said tentatively, "He doesn't look very dark." I was completely taken aback, and not quite sure how to respond. It never occurred to me that she would assume he was black, and it never occurred to her to be bothered that he was. So while his race is a detail I never even thought to mention prior to living in South Africa, it's becoming clear to me that here, it matters.

This place that I will have to learn to consider my home is on the outskirts of Hoedspruit. It's called Ver End (Far End)

Lodge: we're literally at the far end of the Drakensberg mountains. Our cottage is one of six buildings clustered on this property that was once a bustling tourist destination. The owners, Franz and Thelma, are tired of that workload and are slowly winding down the business. They now rent out most of the units to long-term tenants like us. In this context, long-term means six months. Nothing seems very permanent here.

Thelma is an administrator at the local maize-meal factory and looks after the bookkeeping and reservations at the lodge. Franz tells us he used to be a major chef and restaurateur in Johannesburg. Fourteen years ago, he and Thelma decided to leave the city behind and head for Hoedspruit.

Franz built this entire place with his own two hands. What it lacks in architectural precision, it makes up for in character. He now oversees a staff of two: Patrick, who looks after the landscaping and building maintenance; and Lina, the maid. Franz still cooks, but has decided to run the restaurant on a bookings-only basis. He no longer has the energy or the interest to be open for walk-in customers.

By the end of our first day here, Johann and I had already acquired a pet, a friendly little tree squirrel we've named Scrat. At first he approached tentatively, but quickly found his courage when he smelled the pumpkin seeds scattered on the palm of my extended hand. That one small meal secured his trust; the next morning he was crawling all over me, and by afternoon he would jump on my head should I walk by without giving him sufficient attention.

As quickly as Scrat adopted me, so did the landlords. They're insisting that I have dinner with them every night while I'm on my own. Even though they're tired of the hospitality industry, they both thrive on having company. These are really good people, and Johann and I can relax a little knowing they're looking out for me.

I've prepared as best as I can for Johann's departure. I wander into the tiny kitchen and wonder how I'll manage to make a meal here. There's barely enough counter space to lay down a cutting board. I don't have a stove or a microwave, just a two-plate cooker. I take stock of my provisions: rice, pasta and, most importantly, a five-litre box of red wine. I paid R100 for it, which is about 10 Canadian dollars. I know that sounds cheap, but it's a big chunk of my weekly grocery allowance.

It says on the box that this wine is a perfect companion to stews, hamburgers, omelettes, and one of my new favourite dishes, the Malay-inspired traditional South African bobotie, which is a tasty combination of ground beef, chutney and spices, topped with a savoury egg custard.

I hope the cheap red will also pair well with loneliness and anxiety. I didn't invite those guests, but they're already here and I have a sinking feeling that they plan to stick around for the next thirty days.

Once upon a time, in my hectic former life, I craved the opportunity to carve out time to spend alone. My, how things have changed! I wish I could find a way to feel more positive about this, but I'm feeling lonely, isolated and afraid.

I'd hoped that by the time Johann had to leave I would feel more comfortable in my new surroundings. I'm working on my evolution from North American City Dweller to South African Bush Woman but despite my best efforts it's still very much a work in progress.

I've been doing a lot of spiritual reading and exploration over the last few years, and I have come to understand that all emotions are based in either love or fear.

I am learning to love most things about the bush. The majestic marula and syringa trees, the hundreds of species of multicoloured birds and, of course, the reason so many tourists journey here – the uniquely African menagerie of elephant, zebra, giraffe, rhino, hippo, lion, leopard and cheetah. Love for the furry and feathered flows easily.

When it comes to the slithering, scaly and crawly, I remain firmly entrenched in fear. As much as I want that dynamic to change, fear does seem to be a completely reasonable response to these creatures, as some of the snakes, scorpions and spiders here are venomous and can kill you. Sometimes fear is just good sense, right?

But I am making progress. The first time I pulled back the heavy navy-blue curtains in the lounge to let in some light,

I screamed, startled by the gecko that had been taking a nap in their deep folds. I now regard that little fellow as a good friend. He has the night shift covered for mosquito-eating and I'm currently looking for a live-in lizard to keep an eye on things during the day.

I can at least manage an appreciation for all of God's creatures in the wild, but I still lose it when I find a golfball-sized beetle in my bedroom. And don't even get me started on the cockroaches. Like I said, I'm working on it.

Our cottage is spacious and nice in a rustic sort of way, with lots of exposed stone and a red-clay floor. I don't mind rustic, but I do wish it was smaller. I've always preferred small spaces, and when I'm alone, I like to be able to keep an eye on everything from one vantage point. The layout of this place has me more than a bit concerned. I don't like the long dark corridor that separates the bedroom from the rest of the space, largely because the light switch is at the other end of the hallway. Note to self: leave headlamp on bedside table for middle-of-the-night bathroom excursions. Sandals by the bedside too; don't want to risk stepping on anything slimy, scaly or hairy in my bare feet!

The space is more than a bit unusual because it was originally set up as a dorm for the large groups that would occasionally stay here. As a result, we have three toilet stalls (no waiting) and another larger room with a shower, bath and sink. I was thrilled to see the bathtub – a rarity in South Africa in most rentals and hotel rooms. I haven't been able to use it yet, due to a flood a few weeks ago which rendered the water brown with mud. You don't notice it so much in the shower, but bathing in it? Well, they do charge big bucks for mud baths in spas. Maybe I should give it a try.

We'd heard about the flood prior to my leaving Canada but chose to disregard that information and not share it with my family and friends. They were already worried enough that I was moving to the other side of the world.

Truthfully, neither Johann nor I understood the severity of the flooding. Many cars, homes and businesses were swept away by the raging river. Roads were washed out and bridges mangled. Hoedspruit was declared a disaster area. The Red Cross came in to distribute water and whatever else they could muster.

Weeks later, the fact that we're dealing with brown-to-orange water coming from the taps seems only a minor inconvenience. At least there *is* water.

Clean drinking water is available from huge tanks set up in the parking lots of the local grocery stores. The queues can be long, with people from all walks of life bringing plastic bottles, buckets and tin cans to fill. Folks who would otherwise never meet strike up conversations while waiting for their turn at the tap. For this reason, while it is a major inconvenience, I look forward to the water-fetching excursions. They say this could go on for months before things get back to normal.

I wonder if living in Africa will be my new normal by the time the water runs clear again. At the moment, my first thought when I wake up in the morning is, "Oh my God, I live in Africa!" That fact is completely shocking in one way, and yet not surprising at all in another. While I had a wonderful life in Canada and still have a deep appreciation for all my native country has to offer, on a deep level I have always felt connected to this magical continent.

Watching my husband leave today reminded me of another day, some forty years ago, when I stood at the end of a driveway looking down a road. It was a much happier occasion. I was literally jumping with anticipation. I remember I was wearing my favourite dress, the one with the red flowers and bright green leaves. I wanted to look my best. I kept looking down the road, anxiously awaiting the first glimpse of my uncle Ken's car. The old station wagon would be full, carrying him, my aunt, Dad's sister Anita, four of my cousins and the guest of honour, my great-uncle Ernest. The last time I'd seen him I was only five years old, but he was vividly etched in my young mind. As was Africa.

Ernest was a Christian Brother – a male nun, if you will. That doesn't mean he was straightlaced. He enjoyed a good card game and a shot of rye whiskey as much as the rest of the men in our family. It was his calling that set him apart. He was a missionary and primary-school teacher in Nigeria. Every two years he would come home to visit, and for me, his arrival was like all the Christmases and birthdays in between rolled into one joyous event.

Now that happy day was here and the blue car was pulling up alongside me. Uncle Ernest emerged from the front seat and swept me into his arms. I'd never been hugged so hard.

From my seven-year-old perspective, he was larger than life – a big man with a big laugh and an even bigger spirit. He always brought gifts – nut necklaces, bone bracelets and small carvings. I know now that these were cheap tourist souvenirs, but as I child I thought they were more beautiful and valuable than the Crown Jewels. Part of me still does. On this day, he fished in his jacket pocket and produced a tiny ebony elephant with white wooden tusks. It instantly became my most cherished possession.

The family gathered in the living room to listen to Uncle Ernest tell stories. All afternoon I stayed close by his side while he talked about life in rural Nigeria. I wanted to know everything about his home, his school and the children he taught. I was in grade two, and I was excited to find out he was teaching a second-grade class. He talked about his students and showed me some photos of them. They had bright eyes and beaming smiles. They were the same age as me, but our lives were so different. They walked for miles to get to school, and struggled to find paper to write their lessons. Many of them didn't have enough to eat. My great-uncle, my hero, was there to help. I knew there and then that I wanted to be like him, and I would start right away.

After a big family feast, the usual card game began. The four men who were the biggest influences in my young life sat around the small folding table armed with their rye whiskey and their loose change.

Uncle Ray had a distinct advantage in this scenario. While he was a sailor by trade, I think he actually earned more than his monthly salary through gambling. Whenever he got paid, he would find or create a card game and wager his wages. He would wire his winnings home to his steady, dependable elder brother, my dad. Dad would put the money into a special bank account. Whenever Ray had enough saved, he would quit his job and go travelling, spending months exploring different exotic locales. He quite often found himself in Africa.

Whenever Dad, Ken, Ray and Ernest were together, they played a traditional French-Canadian card game called Fifty-Eight. It required more nerve than skill, and Uncle Ken in particular was known for his bravado. The worse the hand he was dealt, the more confidently he'd bid. He loved to take a big risk, or "a flyer", as he called it. I admired that, but whomever happened to be his partner in the game usually did not. Funny thing, though: more often than not, he'd end up winning the hand despite the odds.

I watched the game until Mom said it was time for me to go to bed. She tucked me in and I lay there smiling at the sound of their laughter until I fell asleep.

I woke up the next morning determined to come up with a plan to help the children in Uncle Ernest's class. It was nearly

Easter, so I decided to have an Easter-egg raffle to raise money for school supplies. With the help of my parents and the permission of my teacher, I bought the biggest chocolate egg I could find. It was beautifully decorated with green and yellow icing. I made raffle tickets and sold them to the kids in my class. I raised five dollars, which didn't seem like enough. I asked for more donations and in the end a whopping eight dollars made its way overseas, providing a bit of paper and some pencils for those children who so desperately wanted to learn.

That was the not-so-auspicious beginning of my philanthropic career. I followed it up with a backyard carnival that raised twenty-four dollars and change. Small successes, but they had a big impact on my life. In my own small way, I felt I was following in my great-uncle's footsteps.

Uncle Ernest was the most altruistic person I've ever known. He didn't own anything; he literally would give away the shirt off his back. When he retired, he moved back home to Canada to look after the "old" Brothers in his Order – they were in their 60s; he was in his 80s. When he came back to our cold climate, my mother gave him a winter coat that had belonged to her father. The next time we saw Uncle Ernest, he didn't have the coat. He'd given it to someone who needed it more. My mother was not impressed.

His purpose was to help others. He didn't even keep his meagre salary, always donating it back to the Brotherhood. He lived simply and with the joy that comes from knowing you're exactly where you're supposed to be, doing what you're meant to do.

I want that too. I have a strong feeling that Africa is where I'm supposed to be. I wonder what it is that I'm meant to do. With my husband away, I now find myself with plenty of time on my hands to ponder that.

This is my second sojourn in South Africa, not counting the two-week whirlwind visit where Johann and I surprised everyone, including ourselves, by getting married.

That remarkably rash romantic impulse has birthed this unnerving new reality: I'm half a world away from home, in a country where the culture is completely foreign, and English is only one of eleven official languages. I live 22 kilometres from the nearest town. I have no transportation and little money. To say my internet access is limited is an understatement: buying data is expensive, and out here the signal is unreliable at best.

I have absolutely nothing to do for the next thirty days except possibly have a nervous breakdown. I'll try to hold off on that for as long as possible.

When I think about it, I'm still amazed by my decision to marry a man I barely knew and change my life completely. Now *that's* what I call a flyer!

2

Gordhim, South Sudan

January 2010

Our small Humanitarian Air Services plane began its descent near the tiny village of Gordhim. By all appearances, we were landing literally in the middle of nowhere – an expanse of light-brown dust dotted with trees as far as the eye could see.

As we came closer, I could distinguish grass-roofed huts among the trees. They were hard to see as the colour of the thatching grass blended right in with the dirt. There wasn't a soul in sight.

It looked pretty much as I had expected but until you actually see it, it's hard to grasp just how big, dry and barren the landscape actually is.

This was a trip that I'd wanted to make for several years, and as I examined the path that brought me here, I was left wondering if this was an illustration of the old adage "be careful what you wish for".

I was travelling with a charity called Canadian Aid for Southern Sudan (CASS). I'd been a supporter of the cause for years, no doubt because of the special place that all things

African held in my heart. While I'd always wanted to go on one of the group's aid trips, my job wouldn't allow it. The aid team always went in January, and that's ratings time in the radio industry. I'd been a morning-show host for nearly thirty years, and my contract stipulated that I couldn't take time off during ratings.

Then, suddenly, that was no longer an issue. I'd lost my job.

After nearly thirty years on the air, I was finished. Even as those words registered in my mind again for what seemed like the millionth time, it still didn't make any sense to me. It just wasn't fair. I was good at my job and had devoted my whole adult life to my career. Now it was over.

I gave my head a shake and dismissed the ugly thought. *Be here now*, I admonished myself. *You're finally here, so get out of your head and get into this moment.*

The plane touched down, and suddenly we were surrounded by a cluster of people with the darkest skin and the broadest, most beautiful smiles I've ever seen. They were so joyful and excited about seeing their old friends again.

The founders of CASS, Glen and Jane, had a long history of doing good work here, starting with raising money to buy and repatriate South Sudanese who'd been sold into slavery in the north of the country. The couple had raised enough money to build an elementary school and were working with an organisation called the Water School to teach the villagers how

19

to purify water using only plastic bottles and sunlight. And after having adopted three orphaned children from the community, Glen and Jane were now regarded as family here.

In addition to checking on past projects, the focus of this trip was on building a high school in the area. We were also bringing medicine and music to the village of Gordhim. The people who lived here were still struggling with tuberculosis and other diseases that are no longer issues in developed countries, and the medicine was a delivery of basic supplies from Canadian Partners in Medicine to the local clinic and to a refugee camp near the Darfur border.

The music was in the form of an art and music camp for the local children. The idea was created by my friend Denise, a luminous lady with a big voice and a bigger heart, and her friend Lucy, a gifted self-taught artist and entrepreneur. Brian, an extraordinary musician and composer, was another new addition to the group this year. He'd brought along his guitar to accompany Denise and perhaps teach a few of the children to play.

This was the fourth visit to the village for Denise and Lucy, so as they climbed down the rickety steps of the small airplane, they were quickly engulfed by those who had so anxiously awaited their return. I stood back watching these happy reunions until I was the last one remaining on the plane. As I started down the steps, I felt like I was being drawn into a vortex of joy as my hands were clasped by each of the members of the impromptu receiving line.

"Hello! My name is Peter. You are most welcome here!"

"I am Mark. Welcome, welcome!"

"I am Simon. I am glad you are here!"

It was all quite overwhelming.

We were assisted onto the beds of a few waiting trucks and started our short journey to the parish that would be our home for the next few weeks.

The charity didn't want to spend any of the funds raised on a headquarters; all donations went directly into the projects. When volunteers travelled to Sudan, they were housed by the local nuns and priests. The volunteers paid for their own food, and covered the cost of the extra fuel that would be used to run the generator during their visit.

As we bounced down the dusty dirt road, we were greeted by everyone who saw us pass. The children ran alongside the truck waving, pointing and shouting.

"*Kwaja!*" they cried.

Glen waved and shouted back "*Moonjang!*"

The children were taken aback, but then started laughing.

With a mischievous twinkle in his eye, Glen explained. "*Kwaja* means 'white person', so I respond with *Moonjang*, which is 'black person'. It always catches them by surprise."

We pulled into the church compound and were greeted by some of the nuns and the head priest, Father Benned. Then we heard the sound of rap music blaring from computer speakers, as a man wearing a garish Hawaiian shirt and silver athletic shorts emerged from his room. Father Sebastian apparently liked both his clothing and his music loud.

We were assigned to our rooms. I was pleased to find out I would be staying on the priests' side of the compound. I had a sneaking suspicion that this would prove to be more fun than staying with the nuns.

We unpacked what little we'd brought. We'd kept our personal items to a minimum so that most of the airline weight allotment could be used for the medicine we were delivering. I'd been told that I wouldn't need much in the way of clothing, anyway – shorts, T-shirts and something to wear to church on Sundays would suffice. The real "essentials" were powdered iced tea to mask the taste of the purifying tablets we would put into the water, two-minute noodles, oatmeal and some nuts to add a little variety to the daily rice-and-beans diet.

The next day was Sunday, so we put on our Sunday best and walked across the yard to the church. This building was the heart of this small community and, like the people, it bore the scars of years of civil war. Bombings had left cracks in the walls through which you could see daylight, and there was a gaping expanse between the walls and the ceiling at the entrance. Planks were erected around the door frame to add some stability, but whether or not that made the building structurally sound was anybody's guess.

We were seated in places of honour to the side of the pulpit. The rhythmic drumming began and the congregation's voices soared, literally giving me goosebumps. As I looked out at the assembly, I felt in awe of the joy and hope that radiated from these people. It occurred to me that they knew something we North Americans didn't. I hoped that over the next few weeks they would share their secret.

After the service, we gathered for tea on the long narrow porch in front of the priests' residence. A young man who stood well over six feet came over to me, taking both my hands in his. His name was David; I recognized him as having been part of the greeting committee the day before.

"Jacquie," he said, smiling and looking deeply into my eyes. "How is it?"

I was surprised he remembered my name.

"It's wonderful, David. So nice to see you!" I impulsively reached up to hug him. He had to bend almost in half to return the embrace.

And so it is, whenever you encounter someone in South Sudan. It doesn't matter how many times your paths cross in a day, they will always greet you, and inquire, "How is it now?"

In North America we ask "How are you?" as a social convention, but chances are we won't even look up from our smartphones, much less wait to hear the reply. In South Sudan, when they ask the question, they sincerely want to know the answer.

Here, it's all about contact – hands touching, eyes meeting and souls communicating. These people have virtually nothing, but they give everything of themselves. I have never shaken hands as often as I did when I was in Sudan, and that includes all the greeting I did at the thousands of doors I knocked on during my failed federal election campaign. (I didn't know it at the time, but that misadventure was a stepping stone on the path that brought me to Sudan.)

In Sudan there was great respect for elders, even if that elder was your brother and only a year older. I was amazed that when we were seated in a circle on the plastic chairs on the porch, the children would vacate their chairs and offer their seat to someone older who joined the group.

It seemed there was always a group assembled at the priests' residence, wanting to be near the Canadian visitors to listen to our strange accent and find out about exotic things like snow. One day, when we were gathered for afternoon tea, I looked over and noticed a small boy, probably about three years old, staring intently at my leg. Tentatively, he reached out his hand and gently touched my thigh with his index finger. He carefully moved his finger, tracing the path of the blue vein visible under my very white skin. It dawned on me that he'd never seen a vein before – they're invisible under blue-black skin.

He was completely mesmerised. I asked one of the older boys to explain to him that he had them too, but that he couldn't see them because his skin was so dark. He giggled and shook his head, not sure whether to believe it or not.

The following day was the first day of our art and music camp. Denise had come armed with a bag full of noise-makers – jingle bells, shakers and tiny tambourines. Lucy had the craft supplies – paper, coloured pencils, stickers, glue and feathers. She explained that the crafts had to be carefully planned so that they could be done by a child using only one hand – many of the children who came to us would be balancing a younger sibling on their hip.

Six-year-olds looked after two-year-olds while their mothers spent the day fetching water, finding food and preparing the evening meal. They were the lucky ones. Many didn't have mothers at all, having lost them to diseases like Aids and tuberculosis, or to the civil-war violence that had been occurring in the area for the last sixty years or so. I'd never seen youngsters so desperately in need of play.

On the first day we had about thirty children. Then word spread quickly and it wasn't long before more than a hundred eager souls turned up each day. I became the Play Lady, filling in the transitions between planned activities by teaching the children the words and actions to childhood classics like the hokey-pokey and "Head and Shoulders, Knees and Toes", and leading them in the world's biggest conga line. That experience in itself was life changing.

Then I met the man who would become my husband.

It wasn't love at first sight – it was quite dark and difficult to see any of the people assembled around the campfire that evening. Our group had been invited to dinner at the headquarters of the International Organisation for Migrants (IOM). It was their mission to create an orderly flow of people crossing the border between the Republic of Sudan in the north, and South Sudan.

Many South Sudanese had been displaced by war, famine, fire and even kidnapping. They were now flocking back to take part in the impending referendum they hoped would see South Sudan emerge as a sovereign nation. They knew their northern neighbours didn't want to let them go because it would mean relinquishing control of vast oil reserves. The South Sudanese were desperate to get home to vote because they were afraid that if they cast their ballots in the north, those chits would somehow mysteriously not be counted.

CASS was one of the sponsors of IOM's work. In honour of that, and probably just because they wanted some new people to talk to, they threw a dinner party to welcome us. Also invited to the dinner that night were the de-miners. They were a mostly South African contingent working under a United Nations contract to clear the roads of all the landmines that had been laid through the years of bloody conflict. Johann was hired as a paramedic and he travelled with the de-miners, just in case. Luckily, so far it had been a pretty safe operation and his job had consisted largely of handing out headache tablets and malaria medication.

The South Africans had taken over the grill that night and presented us with a magnificent meal – traditional spiced sausages called boerewors (literally, "farmers' sausage") and possibly the best braaied (barbecued) chicken I've ever tasted.

To avoid hurt feelings, most of our crew claimed to be vegetarians – they were afraid to eat meat in a country where it can easily be 50 degrees in the shade and refrigeration is just a concept.

Not Denise and me, though. Four days of eating rice and beans coupled with the heavenly smell of that chicken forced us to throw caution to the wind. Besides, we had a good supply of Imodium on hand, if necessary. The gamble paid off big time!

That's how the conversation started, with Denise and me raving about this fabulous chicken and asking the "chef" what spices he'd used. Johann was non-specific in his reply and I thought he was being coy about his secret ingredients. About six months later, I found out that he genuinely didn't have a recipe – he'd just grabbed what was on hand and thrown it on the chicken. We've been trying to recreate that recipe ever since.

Johann and Denise were making small talk around the fire, and I was rather preoccupied with my own thoughts while gazing into the flames. My reverie was interrupted when I realized Johann was directing a question at me.

"So what do you think of South Africa?" he asked.

"Uh, in what way?" I stammered, trying to buy a little time before answering what had the potential to be a loaded question.

"What do you think it's like?"

"Well, I know it was colonized by the Dutch and the English, so I guess it's a mix of those traditions, as well as all the black cultures."

"But what do you think it's like? Do you think there are lions wandering down the streets?"

"No! I know you have big cosmopolitan cities, towns and agricultural areas – just like we do. The lions are in the bush."

"So you do know something about it then – not like most of the world."

I must confess at this point I felt a bit irritated. Seriously, there I was, in Sudan. Give me some credit for being a little aware of the world beyond my front door!

So it wasn't love at first sight on my part, but apparently it was love at first *sound* on his. He confided much later that he'd asked me the question so he could hear me speak again. He said he was mesmerized by the sound of my voice, that he thought it was very sexy. This was ironic because he'd been talking with Denise, a singer with a deep, rich, melodious voice, but apparently he only had ears for me. Attraction is a strange and mysterious thing.

It was several days before we met again. This time, the gathering was at our place. It was a farewell party for Glen and Jane. Jane had business to attend to in Nairobi, and Glen had to return to the Canadian capital to resume his duties as a Member of Parliament. The rest of us would stay on in Gordhim for another week.

I was in charge of meat for the dinner, which meant travelling about an hour down the dirt road to the weekly goat and cattle auction. When we arrived, William, who'd driven me, had to ask permission from the elders for me to attend and to take pictures. Luckily, this was granted.

Not only was I the solitary white person there, I was also the only woman. I could tell I was the topic of conversation among several of the older men, and began to feel a bit uncomfortable.

A young boy and his little sister walked by, looking at us curiously. They stopped a few feet away from us, then turned around to come back for another look. William smiled at them and said something in Dinka, the main South Sudanese dialect. They smiled and nodded. They'd never seen a white person before.

William decided that we should wait by the cattle-auction area while we sent a couple of the boys who'd come with us to where the goats were being sold. He thought it was best to have them make the purchase, as he had a sneaking suspicion that the price would go up if the sellers knew the white woman was the buyer. Turns out he was right. The boys brought the first goat back to the truck, and by the time they went back to pick up the second goat, the price had mysteriously increased. We decided one goat would have to do.

As we bounced back along the dirt road with our soon-to-be dinner by my side, I decided that tonight I, too, would be an "honorary" vegetarian. I'd been a meat eater all my life, but after looking into the eyes of that goat, I knew I couldn't possibly eat him.

We human carnivores are funny like that, aren't we? If we look at a herd of cattle, it's beef, but if we meet an individual cow and call her Bessie, there's no way she's going to end up as dinner.

It's the same with groups of people, too. If we look at a class or a race, it's easy to be prejudiced, but when you get to know an individual, it's a different story. The world would be a better place if we could just approach each person as an individual.

As we pulled into camp, the kitchen staff came to claim the main course. I said a quick goodbye to Billy (of course, I'd named him by then) and gave him a look that I hoped would convey my thanks for his inevitable ultimate sacrifice.

I then went to our outdoor shower to see if there was enough water left in the tank so that I might be presentable by the time our guests arrived. (Okay, presentable would be a stretch but just smelling clean would be a huge bonus.) After having a quick shower and putting on a clean tank top, I was ready to greet our guests.

The de-miners were among the first to arrive. The boss, Fred, got out of the truck first. He was small stocky fellow with reddish hair and a beard, a gregarious leprechaun of a man who had done most of the storytelling around the campfire that first night. Then the master griller from that evening emerged from the passenger side. To this day there are two things about my husband that strike me every time I see him: his arresting light-blue eyes and his captivating shy smile.

"Fred, Johann, welcome!" I said, assuming my hostess duties.

Fred greeted me, but Johann stopped dead in his tracks.

"Something wrong?" I asked.

"You remembered my name."

"Yes, of course."

We entered the compound and joined the rest of our group, as well as the resident nuns and priests. Before long, our other guests arrived and it was time for dinner. The nuns brought out the feast consisting of the usual rice and beans, but for this special occasion, they produced a salad of lettuce and tomatoes, and of course, the goat stew.

Before we started the meal, Father Benned asked us to hold hands and join him in a prayer of thanks. With Fred holding my left hand and Johann holding my right, I bent my head to pray, heart bursting with gratitude for the opportunity to be in this part of the world among such remarkable people. When the prayer ended, my left hand was released, but my right hand remained engaged for quite some time.

After dinner Father Sebastian brought out his sound system. Suddenly the party was in full swing, complete with reggae music, dancing and lukewarm beer. Johann stayed by my side all evening, except when I ventured onto the dance floor. He was too shy to join in but was well entertained by our attempts to learn to dance like the locals.

A few hours later, our supply of beer was exhausted and so were we. We walked our guests to the gate and said goodnight.

.

3

Gordhim, South Sudan

January 2010

We saw Glen and Jane off the next morning, and then enjoyed our time singing, drawing and playing with the children. After lunch, Father Benned drove us to the closest city, Aweil, to do a little shopping.

With a population of about twenty thousand at the time, this loud, dirty and crowded place stood in stark contrast to the peaceful little village we'd come from. Judging from the stares we got, it was a conservative place, too, and I wished I'd worn something with sleeves rather than a tank top.

Once we'd finished at the market, Father Benned had a surprise for us. He'd arranged to take us to see a beautiful old church and to meet one of his friends who was the priest in residence there.

The church grounds were a peaceful green oasis in the midst of the chaos of the city. The Father greeted us warmly and gave us a tour of the beautiful old building.

"Before you go, you must meet the Sister," said the priest. "She's been the driving force here for years but has just retired now that she's reached the age of 97."

He escorted us into a small courtyard where this tiny radiant woman sat, gracing us with her beatific smile as we were introduced. She was quite excited to learn that we were from Canada.

"I would love to see Canada! I will go there once I get rid of this," she said, indicating the cane leaning against her chair. "I want to get off the plane using only my own legs."

"When you do, we'll meet you at the airport!" Denise exclaimed.

We stood making small talk for a few minutes. Just as we were about to take our leave, the Sister beckoned me to come closer. I leaned down as she took my hands in hers. She pulled me close until we were cheek to cheek, then she took my face in her hands and looked into my eyes.

"I'm praying for you," she said, her eyes glowing with love. "Not for what I want for you, but for what you want for you. Bless you, my child."

I was caught completely off guard, and tears sprang to my eyes. That was the simple question I couldn't answer. What did I want for me? I pondered the question all the way home.

Once we'd unloaded the supplies, I stood on the porch talking with Denise. I had my back to the gate and didn't hear the truck approaching.

"You have company," Denise said and slipped discreetly off to her room.

Johann climbed out of the truck and greeted me. "I was wondering if it would be alright if Fred and I came by this evening to say goodbye to everyone?" he asked. "We've finished with this area of the road and we'll be moving our camp tomorrow."

"That would be great. See you after dinner." I wondered if he noticed I was blushing.

Johann arrived shortly after 8 o'clock, that wonderful time of the day when we enjoyed the benefit of electricity. For two hours each evening, the generator would pump water from the borehole to refill the holding tank. During that period, the Fathers would enjoy the luxury of television. If there was a soccer game or a rugby match on, dozens of people would congregate at the priests' residence and they would have to move the TV out onto the porch to accommodate the crowd. The power inevitably went off before they got to see who won the game, but that didn't seem to dampen their enthusiasm.

On this particular evening, the television was in the common room and the priests were watching the news. The rest of us were sitting on the porch enjoying our tea when Johann joined the group, taking a seat next to me. I noticed he was alone and I asked where Fred was. Johann made a vague excuse and quickly changed the subject.

We all chatted and laughed until at 10 o'clock, right on cue, when the power was cut and the lights went out. Headlamps and flashlights went on, and in an instant everyone had said goodnight and retreated to their rooms, leaving just Johann and me.

He leaned forward and whispered the words I longed to hear. "I brought you beer."

We grabbed our chairs and planted them next to his truck which was parked by the gate. He reached behind the front seat and produced two cans of warm beer. We sat out under the star-studded African sky, trying to pick out the constellations. My northern-hemisphere stargazing experience was useless; with no North Star or Big Dipper, I was lost. Johann pointed out Orion's Belt overhead.

"See – the three stars in his belt, and then, right there, the three that make up his sword."

We now refer to this night as "our night under the stars". It was the first chance we'd had to have a private conversation. We talked about our lives, our philosophies, our successes and our failures.

Uncharacteristically, Johann did most of the talking. He'd just returned from his two-week leave, which he'd spent at home in South Africa in a futile attempt to salvage his nine-year marriage. He and his wife had previously decided to call it quits, but the guilt he'd felt about their six-year-old son had compelled him to give it one more try. His wife was not of the same mind, however, and told him she planned to proceed with the divorce.

The nature of his work in Sudan meant that Johann was a mostly absent parent. That hadn't always been the case; for the first few years of his son's life, he had been a very hands-on dad, looking after most of the middle-of-the-night feedings and diaper changes. Both parents worked, but their income wasn't enough to sustain the family, which was why Johann had applied for a job as a medic with a de-mining company that had a contract in Sudan. By South African standards, it paid a small fortune: his income went from the equivalent of about $600 a month to nearly $4,000.

The high income came at a high personal cost. It was a difficult lifestyle. He lived in a tent in the semi-desert, coping with the harsh heat of the dry season, and the floods, mud and mosquitoes of the wet season. He was on a three-months-on/two-weeks-off rotation for ten months of the year. But because it took two days of travel each way, he was only at home for ten days every three months. (I asked if it was the long absences that had killed his marriage. He said it was quite the opposite: it had been the time apart that had allowed them to stay together as long as they had.)

Instead of solving their financial woes, the higher income made matters worse in the end. Perhaps to alleviate her unhappiness, his wife comforted herself with material goods, racking up a hefty credit-card debt. They bought a house and car they couldn't afford, and which did nothing to make either of them any happier. Johann knew that leaving the marriage was the right thing to do for himself, but the fact that he would rarely see his son weighed heavily on his heart.

I was so engrossed in his story that I lost track of time and it was close to 1am when the light came on in Father Benned's bedroom. I had a feeling he was waiting for me to go to my room before he went to sleep.

"Thank you for a lovely evening, but I really think I should go in so poor Father Benned can go to sleep," I said, with some regret.

"Yes, I think you're right – he's waiting up for you," Johann replied. "But I must ask: may I please write to you? I feel so comfortable with you. I think I've spoken to you more in the last three hours than I've spoken to anyone in the last three years."

I was so glad that he'd asked. I felt a strong connection to him but thought our meeting would just be a beautiful memory for me when I got home. I gave him my email address. We hugged for a long time, reluctant to let the moment end.

As he drove off, I watched the taillights disappear, thinking that I would never see him again and knowing that I would miss him.

I did see him again – the very next day. As I saw the truck pulling up to the gate, a wave of excitement rushed through me. It was unnerving, and again I could feel myself blushing. I went out to meet him and fought the impulse to fling myself into his arms, settling instead for a quick kiss on the cheek.

"I thought you'd moved camp," I said. "Aren't you over an hour away now?"

"Yes, but I had to come back because I have a serious problem. Your email address doesn't work."

I couldn't believe he'd already written to me, even though he knew I wouldn't be able to read his mail for at least another week, when I got back to Canada.

"Of course it works," I said. "Maybe you just can't read my writing."

"Is that an 'f'?"

"No, it's an 'x'."

"Ah. That would explain it."

"What did you write to me?"

"You'll see."

It was about 4 o'clock, our usual teatime, so we joined the group on the porch. Johann had to get back to his camp before it got dark, so it was a short visit.

When we all walked him to his truck to say goodbye again, I was starting to get a little choked up. So was he.

"Okay, so this really is it," he said to the group with a forced smile. "I'm not coming back to say goodbye to you people again."

Why was I finding it so hard to say goodbye? I supposed that it was because even though I hadn't known him for long, I felt I knew him very well. The only way I could explain it was as soul recognition. I truly saw him, and he truly saw me.

As I watched him drive away again, Denise came and stood beside me, putting her arm around my shoulders.

"You okay?"

"Yeah, just a little sad. I'm never going to see him again."

"You don't know that," she said. "Life is full of surprises."

Our time in Gordhim was quickly coming to an end. We held our final art and music camp, attended by over 150 children. Denise led them in a fabulous farewell performance. By now they all knew the words to the songs she'd taught them, and their joyful voices filled the church.

Our final art project was also a big hit. We passed out drawings of birds, and the children glued on colourful feathers.

For my final activity, we did a reprise of the conga line, singing the words Brian had provided to the basic conga melody. I'm sure that melody still haunts him in his sleep.

Everybody dance now!

Everybody dance now!

Everybody dance now!

Dance, dance the conga!

With so many dancers, we now formed three long lines, headed up respectively by Lucy, Brian and me. Denise led the singing and clapped the conga beat as we did the "one, two, three, kick!", snaking our way around the churchyard. The faces of the children radiated sheer joy. Laughter and music filled the air. We were all caught up in the exhilaration of the moment, and briefly forgot how sad we all were that this would be our last time together. When the song ended, we went through the lines, hugging each child and saying our goodbyes.

When the children left, we went back Into the church and started packing up the instruments and craft supplies. Just then, one of the young men who'd been helping as a translator appeared in the doorway.

Butrus was a gentle, kind soul who loved to help. He was always the first to turn up at the camp every morning, and he'd stay for a few hours until it was time for him to go to school.

When I walked over to greet him, I could tell he was nervous.

"Jacquie, may I speak with you?"

"Of course, Butrus. What is it?"

He hesitated a moment, then found the courage to begin his well-rehearsed speech.

"I am not from here. I lived with my parents on a small island, but there was no school there, so my parents sent me here to live with my aunt and uncle so I could go to school. I am doing very well in my studies. I graduate from elementary school this year, and I want to continue my education. We had no school for five whole years because of the war, so I am 17 years old now, and I do not want to wait to go to high school. There is no high school here, so for me to continue, I have to go to another city, pay school fees, lodging, food and transportation. It is very expensive. I wonder, Jacquie, if you would be able to help me?"

"How much does it cost, Butrus?"

"Seven hundred dollars."

We stood in silence for a moment. Seven hundred dollars. Such a small amount of money in the grand scheme of things, and one that would make such a difference in this young man's life. I struggled hard to find the right words, and harder not to cry.

"The first thing you have to know, Butrus, is how much I want to help you. You deserve this opportunity. The other thing you have to know is that I lost my job. I hope I'll get another one soon, but it's not looking very promising at the moment. I can't give you an answer right now, but please, leave it with me and I'll see what I can do. I promise you, I'll do my best, but if the answer turns out to be no, you mustn't despair. That is the project we're working on right now – to build a high school close to Gordhim so all of you can go. It won't be as fast as you'd like, but please know it will happen."

It was now his turn to swallow hard and fight back tears. He was so disappointed, but so gracious in his acceptance of my reply.

"Thank you for speaking with me. I will see you later."

He shook my hand and walked away.

I stood there feeling utterly helpless. Then I got angry. Really angry. Never before had I experienced such a white-hot, burning fury. It felt like my blood was literally about to boil. If I'd still had my job, I could easily have given him $700 now, and every year until he finished high school. How could they take my job away from me?!

From the moment I was let go from the radio station, I tried to convince myself that it was okay – it was nobody's fault, just chalk it up to the bad economy and tough luck. I actually hugged my boss after he had given me the news, because I felt sorry for him; it seemed like it was as hard on him as it was on me. I didn't feel that way now.

No longer mindful of the fact that I was standing outside the priests' residence, out spewed my entire inventory of profane language, revisiting a few favourites more than a few times. Then the tears started to flow. I hadn't cried about losing my job since the day it happened, probably because I was afraid that if I started, I'd never stop.

I'd chosen my career when I was 12 years old, and I made my radio debut at the age of 17 when I got a part-time job at the local station in Midland, Ontario. The competition had been stiff: the other applicants each already had a year of college under their belts; I was still in high school and had no experience whatsoever.

I was shocked that I managed to make the shortlist after the interviews and was called in for an audition. I arrived at the station and the news director took me into the newsroom. He sat me down at a typewriter and gave me the local newspaper and some international stories that had come in over the newswire. I had forty-five minutes to select the stories I thought were most interesting, rewrite them, and put them in what I thought was the right order to create a five-minute newscast.

I sorted through the stories and started writing as quickly as I could. I finished in forty minutes, then took the last five to read over the copy, checking for words that might trip up my tongue as I tried to deliver the newscast.

When the allotted time was up, the producer came to get me. My legs felt weak and shaky as I stood up from the workstation and followed him into the tiny recording booth. I'd never been so nervous before, and I don't think I ever have been since. I settled into the chair, put on the headphones and adjusted the microphone. I didn't know how far away it should be from my mouth, but I didn't want to ask for fear of looking like the complete amateur I was.

The producer sat facing me on the other side of the huge window that separated the booth from the studio. In my headphones I could hear him count down: *three*, and every bit of saliva in my mouth evaporated instantly; *two*, and it felt like there was a hundred-pound weight sitting on my chest; *one*, and the on-air light flashed red – and a miraculous thing happened. I wasn't nervous any more. I read that newscast like I'd been doing it all my life. They said I was a natural.

I got the job, and I loved it. There was something exciting about getting up in the wee hours of the morning and driving through town while everyone else slept. I looked forward to being the first to find out what had happened in the world overnight and share the news.

I was the weekend anchor, with reporting duties during the week. Attending town-council meetings awakened my interest in politics. Covering hard news gave me a thrill like I'd never experienced. When one of the local factories went on strike, I dashed across the picket line and snuck in to try to get an interview with management. They weren't feeling too talkative and I was physically escorted out the front door and thrown face-first into a snow bank. What an adrenaline rush!

I'd found my calling. I went to college in Toronto to study radio, television and film, and made the two-hour trip back to Midland every weekend to run the newsroom.

Broadcasting was my passion. It gave me a platform to entertain, educate and serve my community.

About a year after I graduated, I got the call I'd been hoping for. Someone who worked at a radio station on the outskirts of Toronto had been visiting relatives in our little town, and when he heard me, he called his boss to tell him that he'd found a girl who was ready to move to the big smoke. I was hired as a traffic reporter, warning drivers about accidents and delays they should avoid as they undertook their daily commutes from suburbs to city and back again.

Truthfully, the job was pretty boring except for when it gave me an opportunity to interact with the drive-time hosts. Verbal sparring with quick-witted guys turned out to be my forte.

My boss called me in to his office one day to tell me he was taking me out of the newsroom. I asked if I'd done something wrong.

"No," he said. "You're funny. I want to make you a co-host."

I had a great career; interesting and challenging. And it came with perks – everything from free concert tickets, where I was actually up on stage introducing the performers, to Caribbean cruises where I entertained contest winners and clients. I rode in limousines and wore expensive evening gowns as the host of charity galas. It was a lifestyle I could never have afforded on my salary.

For three decades, I lived an extraordinary life. Now, as I stood in the glare of the scorching Sudanese sun, I was forced to admit once and for all that it was over.

Even the biggest storms eventually pass, and of course you really can't cry forever. The tears stopped and I leaned back against the brick wall. I closed my eyes and slumped down on the concrete porch. I was physically, mentally and emotionally drained. Butrus's small request had broken the dam I'd so carefully built to keep my emotions in check, and now that the torrent of feelings had spilled out, I needed to find some calm.

I sat still and tried to focus on my breath. I wished I was better at meditating. I struggled not to fidget. Finally, a phrase came into my mind: "find the blessing" – no doubt something I'd picked up from one of the dozens of self-help books I'd read in the last year.

Okay, what's the blessing here?

Nothing leapt to mind.

I kept my eyes closed, still concentrating on my breath.

What is the blessing?

My mind stubbornly refused to cooperate.

Eventually, I settled on this: *If I hadn't lost my job, I wouldn't be here. And because I'm here, I met Butrus, and he's asking for my help. I must find a way to help him, and that will be a blessing for both of us.*

I got up and went to find Denise.

"How was your chat with Butrus?" she asked. "Did he ask you what I think he asked you?"

"He wants me to sponsor him for school."

"I figured that's what was up when he asked to speak to you. They assume we all have lots of money. You can't blame them."

"No, of course not. By comparison, we *do* have lots of money. That's what makes this so hard."

"Yes, but Jax, you're not in a position at the moment to fork out money."

"I know, but maybe we can find a way. Do you have any money left?"

"About a hundred bucks. You're welcome to it."

"I have about the same. Let's go see Brian."

When we explained our plan, Brian couldn't reach into his pocket fast enough. We now had almost half of what we needed.

We sent one of the boys to find Butrus. A few minutes later, he appeared in the doorway. There was sweat on his brow and he was still trying to catch his breath.

"You wanted to see me?" he asked.

"Yes," I replied. "We want you to know that we believe in you, and we want to support you. Here's the money for the first semester. We'll go home and raise the rest and send it to you in time for the second semester."

Shock and disbelief, then relief, registered on his face in quick succession. Then he grinned, his eyes beaming with happiness and gratitude. He hugged each of us in turn, then gathered us all in for a group hug. We were jumping up and down, laughing uncontrollably.

"Thank you, thank you, thank you!" he cried. "I will make you proud."

"You already have," I said.

4

In transit

January 2010

The time had come to leave our friends in Gordhim and none of our group was looking forward to the return trip. It was a three-day trek via Amsterdam to reach my home in the city of London in southwestern Ontario, Canada. Just to get out of Sudan, we had to take a small plane to Juba, then another to Lochie, where we boarded a slightly larger craft to travel to Nairobi in Kenya, where we would meet up with Jane.

What better way to celebrate the end of our Sudanese rice-and-beans diet than to go to a Nairobi restaurant called Carnivore? We sampled everything on the menu from alligator, which was tough and dry, to tender tasty ostrich, which is more like steak than fowl. Of course, none of us slept well that night after completely gorging ourselves. We were amazed at how our stomachs had shrunk during our time in Sudan.

We were all up early the next morning, eager to take advantage of the only day we had to do a bit of sightseeing and souvenir shopping. We went on a somewhat disappointing game drive, which saw us meandering around one of the national parks for a few hours with only a few antelope and a baboon putting in an appearance to reward us for our trouble. Then we drove out to the Karen Blixen Museum on the grounds of the estate the Danish author made famous in her romantic autobiography *Out Of Africa*. I enjoyed the tour of the museum, but I was particularly anxious to get to the gift shop. Since meeting Johann, my interest in romance had been rekindled, and I was on a mission.

At our wedding over ten years before, my former husband and I had been given a pair of porcelain figures as a gift: the graceful lacquered silhouettes of an African man and woman, both on bended knees. They were separate, but they sat face to face, and they were bending slightly, seemingly in reverence to each other. We'd put them in a prominent spot, on the fireplace mantel in our living room.

Mere months into our marriage, as I sat curled up on the couch by the fire, reading, the male figure had suddenly toppled over, as if pushed by an invisible hand. As I stared in disbelief at the shards on the floor, it occurred to me that this might be an omen. As it turns out, it was.

Now maybe I could make it work in reverse. If I could find similar figures that were actually joined together, maybe a lasting relationship would follow. I scoured the curio shop in vain. There were figures that had the same look about them, but none that were joined. For the rest of the day, I checked in every shop and booth we passed, but with no luck. I decided maybe I wasn't superstitious after all.

It had been a long day, and we were all tired by the time we got to Nairobi airport to catch our overnight flight to Amsterdam. We had a little time to kill, so I decided to have a browse in the duty-free shops. I tried a few perfumes and checked out the liquor – some good bargains, but really nothing worth trying to get back to Canada in one piece.

I was about to head back to the boarding lounge when a shop brimming with carvings caught my eye. I decided to give it one last try. I walked in and said hello to the young man behind the counter – and immediately saw, on the shelf over his left shoulder, the carving I'd been looking for. It was a man and a woman, fashioned together out of one piece of wood. They stood face to face, heads inclined, with foreheads touching. The space between their faces was nearly heart shaped. Their arms were wrapped around each other's waist.

The words "I'll take it" were out of my mouth before I even thought to ask the price.

The flight to Amsterdam was uneventful, and when we arrived we settled in for the long layover – we had eight hours to wait before our final flight to Toronto. I started feeling restless and anxious. I was on my way home, but what was I going home to? My career and my marriage were over, both brought to an end indirectly as the result of a decision I'd made a few years earlier. I'd decided to run for office on a national scale.

My work in media, particularly in news, had made me acutely aware of politics and its impact on all of us. People often express disdain for politics, saying "It has nothing to do with me", when in fact the opposite is true. It has everything to do with each of us, and if we don't get involved, we end up being represented by people who don't reflect who we are.

The political climate in Canada had started to change leading up to the 2006 election that saw the Conservative Party come into power. It seemed to me that we were moving away from the compassionate values and policies that had made me proud to be a Canadian. The world had once seen us as negotiators and peacekeepers, but that reputation was fading fast.

I watched the 2006 Liberal Party leadership convention with great interest, and when the new leader was elected, his victory speech was a call to action. He was looking for new candidates, particularly strong female candidates, as women were vastly underrepresented in Parliament. I felt compelled to come forward.

So many factors discourage people, and women in particular, from going into politics. It takes an extraordinary amount of time, energy and money. To enter public life while trying to raise a family requires a huge sacrifice on the part of the candidate as well as her spouse and children. I didn't have children, and it seemed to me that my reputation for contributing to my community, along with the name recognition generated by my broadcasting career, made me a likely candidate. I discussed this with my husband of seven years.

"I really feel I need to do this," I explained. "There are so many women who can't run for office but I can and I want to. As corny as it sounds, I think I can make a difference. Will you support me in this?"

"If that's how you feel, then that's what you should do," he replied.

My first call was to Glen who, in addition to his work for South Sudan and as the director of the local food bank, was also a Member of Parliament. I admired him greatly, and his example was a big part of my inspiration to become more politically involved.

I met him for coffee and explained the reasons why I wanted to run alongside him in the next federal election. I could tell he didn't want to dampen my enthusiasm, but he was hesitant to encourage me. He chose his words carefully.

"That's all admirable, and it would be great to have you on the team, but as a friend, Jacquie girl, I have to ask: are you sure you want to do this? I think you're too nice to be in politics."

"You're probably the nicest person I know!" I countered.

"And I'm finding it more difficult than I can say," he replied with a sad smile.

Despite Glen's warning, I launched the campaign to win the nomination for my party. It was the beginning of what would turn into a two-year odyssey.

I was elected as the Liberal candidate in my area, London Fanshawe, and would run in the next federal election. This was at a time when sentiment in the country seemed to be becoming increasingly Conservative. It was pointed out to me by a veteran national-campaign staffer that running as a Liberal at that time was akin to running into a burning building. I had to concede that was true, but it begged the question: what happens if we just let the building burn?

Politics in general had degenerated into a partisan power struggle it was never meant to be, and that had to change. It seemed to me that the only way to change it was for people who weren't "typical" politicians to get involved. Unfortunately, the opposite now seems to be happening, and people are feeling disillusioned and giving up on the process. Democracy may indeed be broken, but as Sir Winston Churchill so famously put it, "It is the worst form of government except all the others that have been tried."

I began canvassing in cold snowy January with a small but very dedicated group of volunteers. Because the government of the day was in the minority in Parliament, we had no way of knowing when the opposition parties would band together to force another election, so we set out to simply reach out to as many voters as possible by knocking on as many doors as we could. By the time Canadians went to the polls in October 2008, we'd knocked on nearly twenty thousand of them.

We trudged through snow that eventually melted and turned the ground to mud as winter turned to spring. We spent scorching summer Saturday afternoons pounding the steaming pavements.

Every time you knocked on a door, you wondered what kind of a reception you would get. Canadians are known for being nice, and thankfully most were. Of course, there are always exceptions. On a couple of occasions, I was yelled at and had doors slammed in my face.

Two incidents in particular stand out in my mind.

We'd been canvassing for hours one summer evening, and it was starting to get dark. We were about to call it a night, but I decided to knock on one more door. A 40-something-year-old woman answered and, recognizing me, smiled brightly.

"Oh, I know you! You're the Liberal candidate," she said. "I really enjoy listening to you on the radio but I won't vote for you because I support another party. But you'll be glad to know that my daughter has just turned 18 and will be voting for the first time. She did research on all the candidates, and she's decided to vote for you. I'm sure she'd love to speak to you. Shall I go get her?"

"Yes, please," I said. "I'd love that!"

She summoned her daughter and the three of us had a stimulating discussion about the high cost of university and the high youth unemployment rate. When I said goodbye, I walked away from the house thinking that maybe I wouldn't win the election, but perhaps because of that conversation, some day that bright young woman might decide to get involved in politics. That thought gave me the incentive to carry on.

The other incident wasn't so encouraging, but it was funny. The election was only a few days away and our fearless leader had been taping a television interview when disaster struck. French was his first language, and the interview was being conducted in English. The reporter asked a question which, due to either exhaustion or the language barrier, the leader misunderstood. His answer made absolutely no sense in the context of the question, and the media had a field day with the clip. It was played over and over, and he was ridiculed mercilessly.

With only two days left until the election, we hit the streets to do as much damage control as possible. I walked up some stairs to a grey stone house in one of the more affluent neighbourhoods in the area. When I rang the bell, an older man opened the door, took one look at my telltale red coat, and said simply, "Liberal."

"Yes."

"Sorry about the guy who leads your party."

"Me, too," I replied matter-of-factly.

There was silence for a moment and then we both burst out laughing.

Election Day was a complete disaster. My friend Glen was one of the few Liberals to retain his seat, but I failed to win mine. I didn't even come close. All that time, effort, emotion and energy invested, and for what? I'd hoped to do so much good for so many, but now it seemed all I'd done was sabotage my own life.

The middle of the election campaign turned out to be the beginning of the end of my marriage. I don't blame politics for it because we truly weren't well suited, but the experience of going through the campaign definitely served to highlight the differences in our personalities and priorities. We agreed to separate – or at least I thought that was the agreement. But when my husband asked for his portion of the assets and went out and put a down payment on a house of his own, it became clear that working at the relationship wasn't part of his plan.

By the time the election campaign was over, after all the stress and emotional turmoil, and finally the complete upheaval brought about by the divorce, I was exhausted. I felt utterly defeated in every way. I was grateful to be able to go back to the one thing in my life I could count on: my career.

It turns out Fate had a trick up her sleeve on that score, too.

Some months later, just when it seemed things were getting back to normal, I got an email from my boss asking me to report to his office after my morning show. When I walked into the room, the human resources manager was sitting there – never a good sign. And indeed it turned out that the show I'd just finished would be my last. The next thing I knew, I was being escorted from the building. Nothing like adding insult to injury, is there?

Radio-station management said it was due to the recession and that I was part of a "downsizing" but the truth is it's never wise for a media personality to declare a political stripe – unless, of course, you're a right-wing talk-show host.

Before my undignified departure from the station, I was required to meet with a career consultant. He gave me his card, along with a pamphlet detailing the do's and don'ts of how to get through the day after being fired. Some of the handy tips: have someone drive you home; don't spend the day alone; avoid alcohol.

Naturally, I got in my car, drove home, locked the door, and poured myself a strong vodka and tonic. And then another.

It's true that misery loves company, so eventually I called a couple of friends who I hoped might help me somehow. One happened to be a damned fine litigator – it says exactly that on his business card – so I asked him to look over the severance package. I guess I was hoping it was flawed and we could contest it. He concluded, however, that it wasn't worth the time, stress or expense to fight for more. In the long run, I'd be better off taking what they were prepared to give and moving on with my life.

I signed the papers and accepted the offer.

That part was easy but how was I going to move on with my life? I didn't have a clue. Not only had I lost my job, but I felt I'd lost my identity. While I'd always tried to separate who I was from what I did for a living, after nearly three decades as a public person, the two were completely intertwined.

I was at loose ends, and floundering emotionally. I desperately needed something, anything to reignite my passion.

Then, as so often is the case in life, an opportunity appeared right out of the blue. I was offered the chance to accompany my friend Mary to Los Angeles to attend a song-writers' convention. She was supposed to go with her husband, but he was on a deadline to finish the score for a television programme. The admission to the conference was already paid for, as was the hotel room. All I had to pay for was the flight.

It was on that trip that I met probably the most spiritual person I'd ever encountered. Originally from Ghana, he now made his home among the rich and famous in Los Angeles, I suspect acting as a spiritual advisor to some of them. He was someone Mary had known for a few years, and we'd arranged to pick him up at the Malibu mansion where he was staying – the home of a music-industry icon.

We announced our arrival over the intercom and waited at the front gate. We strained to get a glimpse of the mansion as the gates swung open to let The Guru out, then closed again. He got into the car next to Mary. She introduced us and we shook hands. He studied me for a moment, then said, "You have a very symmetrical face."

He then turned to Mary and the two of them chatted about mutual acquaintances and music. I listened with great interest but didn't have much to contribute to the conversation. Despite that, it didn't take him long to get a read on me.

When we settled in to have lunch, he turned his attention to me. He gazed thoughtfully at me for a moment, then asked, "What is it you think you have lost?"

"Let's see," I said, trying to make light of it. "My marriage, an election, my career, and I'm pretty sure my house is going to be next."

"You have lost nothing," he said.

"Nothing? Really? It doesn't feel like nothing. To me, it feels like pretty much everything."

"This is what you must understand. Those things were in your life because they served you for a while, but they no longer serve you, so they are no longer there. Those things are not what you are missing, anyway. You are missing the feeling of being in control of your life. But you never had control of your life because none of us does. All you had was the illusion of control. What is an illusion? It is nothing. Therefore, you have lost nothing." He paused for a moment to let that sink in, before adding, "Now you are free to find everything."

Two years later, sitting in Schipol airport in Amsterdam waiting for my connecting flight to Canada, I realized that that was my job now: to go home and find everything.

At long last, our flight was called and we filed on to the plane for the penultimate leg of the trip; the final one would be the two-hour drive to London, where our loved ones would be waiting. Except no one would be waiting for me. My parents lived a four-hour drive away in the small town of Penetanguishene, and neither my elder sister Michele nor my younger sister Giselle lived any closer. Several of my friends had offered to come and get me, but it seemed silly to impose when Denise's sister was taking her home and had offered to drop me off along the way.

I swallowed hard and tried not to feel sorry for myself, but didn't succeed.

5

London, Ontario, Canada

January 2010

It was already dark when I said my goodbyes to Denise and her sister as they dropped me off at the foot of my snowed-in driveway. I couldn't bear the thought of shovelling and decided it could wait until morning.

I trudged through the white stuff and slowly climbed the four stairs leading to my front door. My luggage was light. Before I'd left Sudan, I'd given away most of my clothing, my shoes, my bedding and my flashlight – items so easily replaced here, but so precious to my new friends.

I stood on the porch appreciating the silence and admiring the sparkle of the snow under the streetlights. I stayed there for a long time, but it was cold and there was no point in further delaying the inevitable. I inserted the key in the lock and the door slowly swung open, creaking loudly. The house was dark, empty and very cold.

I stepped inside and closed the door behind me. The silence was devastating.

I located the light switch and flicked it on. I cranked up the thermostat. The green answering-machine light was blinking, but I felt no urgency to check messages. Instead, I got undressed and stepped into the shower. As I stood there, enjoying the luxury of warmth and good water pressure, I wondered how many times in my life I'd stood under a miraculous stream of hot water and taken it for granted. How many times had I flipped on a light switch and thought nothing of it? Are you cold? Turn up the heat. Too hot? Turn on the air. It was all so simple on this side of the world. Being born here was like winning the lottery without even buying a ticket.

I wondered if my new awareness would last, or if I'd go back to taking all of this for granted in a matter of a few months, a few weeks, or even just a couple of days. I hoped not.

I knew I should be feeling nothing but grateful and blessed, but the truth was I felt empty and sad. I went to bed hoping that somehow things would look brighter in the morning.

The sun was shining when I woke so things did in fact look brighter, but I felt no better.

Coffee. Real coffee. That might help.

I made a pot, poured a cup and sat on the couch. I stared out the window, mesmerized by the dazzling snow blanketing the ground.

Three hours later, I still hadn't conquered my inertia. The trip to Sudan had been my focus for the last several months. Now the trip was over and I had to start rebuilding my life. The prospect seemed overwhelming. I truly didn't know where to start.

Then I remembered the list.

Not long before I left for Sudan, I'd been feeling pretty low, and it occurred to me that I was spending far too much time alone. I picked up the phone and arranged to meet a friend for a drink. After she'd patiently listened to my tale of woe, she tried to spur me to action.

"Make a list," she said, "of one hundred things you want in a partner."

She swore that this was the way to find the man of your dreams: make the list, and he will appear.

One hundred things seemed like a pretty tall order, but it seemed to have worked for her, so I figured I'd give it a try. Really, what did I have to lose?

Where to begin? The most important traits, I guessed, were to be loving, kind and honest, to have a good sense of humour, to be passionate and compassionate, to be confident, intelligent, adventurous and ambitious, to be sensitive, loyal and creative. That was only thirteen things, and it seemed like more than enough to build a relationship on.

No, she insisted. You need to get to one hundred.

Generous, fun, attractive, easygoing, wise, witty, charming, dependable, open, supportive, trustworthy, consistent, thoughtful, faithful...

"Keep going," she urged. "Think of smaller things."

"Okay. Loves nature, likes to cook, loves music, especially jazz – can that count for two? – enjoys red wine..."

Eventually I got to the magical number. "Wow, that's a lot of attributes," I observed. "Could a person like that actually exist?"

"Yes," she assured me. "She does. It's you! When you do this exercise, you tend to write down the qualities you have, and now that I've reminded you of how fabulous you are, stop feeling sorry for yourself and go out and find a great partner who shares all the same traits."

Where had I put that list? I went into my bedroom and riffled through the drawers until I found it. I started checking off all the qualities Johann seemed to possess. He wasn't a perfect match for all of them, but he seemed to have all the really important ones. I wondered if he could learn to love jazz...

Then it occurred to me how ridiculous this all was. He was half a world away, and I really didn't know him that well.

I looked at the clock and realized that I'd already wasted more than half the day.

"Okay. Enough," I said out loud. "Stop wasting time. Do something!"

There were phone calls that I should have made – my parents would be anxious to hear from me – but I really didn't feel like talking to anyone. Instead, I turned on the computer to check my email. Thirty-six messages – mostly junk mail, because my friends all knew I was away.

Then my heart leapt. I saw Johann's name. The subject line read, "Hope you are home safe."

I opened the mail to find a diary of each day since we'd parted. It began with, "Hello Lady with the Sexy Voice," and ended three pages later with this closing:

Okay, this is now the final word of goodbye. I just find it hard to say goodbye to you, even in a letter.

Now this is definitely final.

Looking forward to your reply.

Kind regards and good memories

Johann

PS. I really did miss you these couple of days. I just wanted someone to talk to. Not just everyday stuff, but really talking to someone.

That was the beginning of our five-month correspondence which in the end totalled more than six hundred emails and text messages. Our communication was so frequent, intense and personal that in the beginning I was sure it couldn't possibly last.

We had long written conversations about potentially explosive topics like politics and religion. We also shared our personal stories and our feelings in more depth and detail than either of us had ever shared with anyone before.

One day, I was helping out in my friend's home-furnishings store when my cellphone rang. I immediately recognized the deep voice with the sexy South African accent. I could hardly breathe, much less compose an intelligent sentence.

"Love?" he said. "Is something wrong?"

I managed to squeak out, "No, I'm fine, I'm just so surprised you called."

"Well, I wanted to hear that sexy voice again. I'll write to you later."

His intelligence and humour shone through in all of our communication. You have to be very smart to be funny in a language that isn't your own – Johann was raised speaking Afrikaans, but his command of written English was so good I'd often forget that it wasn't his first language.

His sex appeal was also evident. Any man who can make your heart race with a two-sentence text message definitely has it going on. He'd often send me love songs that he felt would do a better job of expressing his feelings than he could write himself.

For my part, it was like the first time I'd ever fallen in love. Then, I was 15 years old, and I gave my heart away with complete abandon, blissfully unaware of just how much it would hurt when that relationship crashed and burned.

Now, despite being significantly older and theoretically wiser, I'd fully offered my heart once more. I'd wake up in the middle of the night to see if there was any word from Johann. He was my first thought in the morning and my last thought at night, and he occupied the majority of my thoughts in between. I was acting like a lovesick teenager. It was by turns exhilarating, painful and terrifying to feel that way again.

When Johann was in an area with internet access, I'd receive three or four mails a day. When he was in a remote location with no internet, he would drive around until he found a phone signal to send a text message. Over the next five months, there were only two days he didn't manage to contact me.

His determination and commitment were obvious – but could this really be love? We had to figure that out. We couldn't possibly go on this way for much longer. The distance between us was too great, and neither of us had the money to be flying back and forth between continents.

As always, I turned to my trusted friends for advice. Most were incredibly supportive. Caroline was all for it. Having been diagnosed with terminal cancer a year earlier, her philosophy was to live for today and seize every opportunity life has to offer.

Marita was also cheering me on. I'd expected the demise of her marriage to make her cynical, but it had actually had the opposite effect. She'd become an incurable romantic.

A few of my friends were apprehensive, however. Johann's financial situation was bleak, to say the least, and as Sarah observed, "Love is great, but you really can't live on it. You have to be practical. At the end of the month, the rent has to be paid, and someone has to put the sandwiches on the table."

My mind knew that my dear friend was right, but my heart wouldn't listen to reason.

Some friends I consulted were downright suspicious. Was this man using me to come to Canada? I had to consider that possibility.

I knew I was vulnerable. There'd been so much change and upheaval in my life. I had to wonder if I was allowing myself to be swept away by this romance just because it felt so good.

I read and re-read his letters, looking for any red flags. I could find none. His words were honest, sweet and sincere. This man who'd met me in the middle of nowhere, unemployed and looking my absolute worst, saw nothing but what was best in me.

Could it be real? Why not? Why couldn't it be love?

I had to go to South Africa to find out. Johann couldn't come to Canada – visitors' visas for South Africans weren't readily granted, as so many people were anxious to find a way to try their luck at starting a new life in North America. With his profile – 39 years old, divorced, and with only a contract job – Johann would be viewed by Immigration as a risk and likely not be allowed into the country. But I could easily go to South Africa without any red tape at all.

Just prior to my departure, my parents came to visit me. They were supportive but clearly anxious about my impending trip. In our many email exchanges, Johann and I had discussed this, and he wanted to try to find a way to reassure them of his integrity and his honourable intentions toward their daughter. On the morning they were due to arrive, a note arrived in my email inbox, and it had an attachment. It was a letter from Johann, addressed to my parents.

We were settled in the living room after dinner when I handed my mother the letter. She read it aloud.

Dear Mr and Mrs Gauthier

I hope you are enjoying the warmer summer weather in Canada. I have never experienced it, but I understand it can be very cold there.

I am writing this letter to you in the hope that I can convince you of my sincere intentions towards your daughter. I know that it must be difficult for you to believe that we can have these strong feelings for each other after being in each other's company for such a short time, but I assure you I have never felt so strongly about anyone before.

Your daughter is the most amazing woman I have ever met and I asked myself about a hundred times why she would be interested in someone like me. She has done many things in her life and achieved many things others can only dream of and yet she is a down-to-earth person with an amazing amount of compassion and understanding for other people.

I love Jacquie very much, and I truly believe we will be very happy together.

I believe in fate, so I feel I was meant to meet Jacquie at this time in my life. I think she is the most special person on this planet. I am one hundred percent dedicated to her and to this relationship. She is the best thing that has ever happened to me, and I am not going to let it slip out of my hands.

We only met four times when we were both in Sudan, but it was enough for me to know that she is different from anyone else I have ever met. I normally find it quite difficult to communicate with someone I don't know, but with Jacquie it was different. I found it very easy to talk to her and I cannot get over how natural it felt when we were together. I was not planning or hoping to meet anyone new (and especially not in Sudan, of all places) but I am very happy that we did meet.

I would really like to meet you both too. Under normal circumstances it would be appropriate for a man to meet his sweetheart's parents at this stage.

Thank you for taking the time to read my letter and I hope you will feel better knowing that I really care for your daughter and I really believe she is the one I have been searching for my whole life.

Best regards

Johann

Shortly after my mother finished reading, my father rose and quickly said goodnight, probably because he needed some time to process his feelings. He's not one to react hastily – or sometimes at all – where emotion is concerned.

My mother and I stayed up late into the night, talking about my feelings for this man and what they might lead to.

"Do you think you might marry him?" she asked.

"Maybe."

"On this trip?"

"I won't know until I see him again."

It was something Johann and I had discussed but there was no way to predict what might happen. Perhaps we'd discover that we'd been swept up in a fairytale romance that wasn't real and couldn't be sustained; or we might feel certain that this was a rest-of-your-life love. It could go either way and I didn't know which outcome to hope for.

If we didn't connect in person and the chemistry wasn't there, we'd agreed we'd just have a nice holiday together and remain friends. That would be simple.

But if it was love?

That would be complicated. Very, very complicated.

I did one last sanity check before I left – sometimes it's very convenient having a psychiatrist in the family. My elder sister, Michele, assured me that there was nothing crazy about going to see him again.

"If you don't," she said, "you'll always wonder."

The 23-hour flight from Toronto to Johannesburg seemed interminable. To pass the time, I read and half-watched a couple of movies, but it was hard to keep my mind on anything except what might happen when I got there. When we'd said goodbye in Sudan, Johann and I knew there was an attraction.

Now, half a year later, we were in love – on email, anyway. What would it be like when we saw each other again?

As the plane began its descent, my heartbeat accelerated and a knot formed in my stomach. Panic was definitely setting in. My thoughts were screaming: *What am I doing here? Have I completely lost my mind? Am I seriously willing to leave behind everyone and everything I know? Most people would just enjoy a little romance in an exotic place, and then go back to their lives. Who gets on a plane and flies to South Africa?!*

Apparently, I do.

I passed through customs and into the commotion of the hundreds of happy reunions. For a brief moment, it occurred to me that maybe he'd changed his mind, that he wouldn't be there to pick me up.

Then I saw him.

I took a deep breath and attempted a detached critical assessment. Not quite as tall as I remembered. Build on the slight side.

Then he saw me and his face lit up. Oh, those incredible blue eyes and that beautiful smile! I felt a surge of warmth rush through my body. *Is this my future husband?*

He walked over to me as I fumbled with my bags. He took me in his arms and we hugged for a very long time – probably because neither of us knew what to say. Johann is normally a man of few words, and he had the peculiar effect of rendering me speechless. We were both nervous, and I became uncharacteristically shy.

He took my luggage and steered me toward the parking garage.

"I must prepare you for the car," he said. "This is not the car I meant to pick you up in, but mine broke down on the highway this afternoon. It's been towed and I don't know how long it will take to repair. In the meantime, we have this," he said indicating a beaten-up white Opel Corsa with a cracked windshield.

I couldn't help but wonder, *Is it midnight, Cinderella?*

6

Johannesburg, South Africa

July 2010

We set out on the highway bright and early, leaving the sprawling city of Joburg behind and heading northeast to Limpopo.

My stomach was churning. Was it nerves? Anxiety? Excitement? Fear? All of the above? Were we brave and sure, or reckless and delusional? We'd been together just a few days, and here we were, heading north to a tented safari camp where we would become man and wife.

Just two days before, it had been the furthest thing from my mind.

After Johann had picked me up at the airport, the drive to the guesthouse was awkward, the strained silence punctuated with bits of small talk about the length of the flight, airplane food, and how dangerous it was to drive in Johannesburg. I was starting to think that coming here had been a big mistake and I seriously considered asking him to turn the car around and take me back to the airport.

Eventually, we arrived at our destination, a little guesthouse in the hamlet of Irene south of Pretoria, half an hour and a world away from the noise and danger of Johannesburg. We checked into our room and had a glass of wine. This wasn't getting any easier, and again I wondered if I could get myself booked on to the next flight back to Toronto.

Finally, Johann took my hand and said, "What's wrong, love?"

"I just don't feel like we're connecting," I said, trying to sound calmer than I felt.

"Give it time, love. It's the first day. You're tired, and we're both a little nervous. I'm sure in a couple of days it will seem like we've been together forever."

And he was right. Here we were, two days later, and not only did it seem like we'd always been together, we knew we wanted it to stay that way. It seemed a bit crazy even to us, but we'd decided to get married.

I must admit that I had second thoughts. Third, fourth and fifth ones too, all stemming from Johann's financial situation. He'd recently wrapped up a nasty divorce, and on the second day we were together, he showed me the agreement. We'd just returned to the guesthouse after a wonderful day of sightseeing around Pretoria.

I was sitting on the bed when he handed me the papers and said, "Read this before you decide if you want to go through with the wedding."

A quick scan of the document showed that he and his ex-wife had amassed a substantial pile of debt, and by court order he was solely responsible for every cent of it. On top of that, he'd been saddled with onerous alimony payments for his ex-wife in addition to the child support I'd expected. These amounts had been determined while Johann had still had a good paying job in Sudan, but a month later, the company had lost the de-mining contract, and he was unemployed. Johann would have to go back to court to change the agreement, but there was no way of knowing how long that would take, or what the judge would decide.

I finished reading the legaleze, stood up, went into the bathroom and threw up.

Kneeling on the floor, I rested my forehead on the cool porcelain and took stock of the situation. It was not looking good. Both of us were unemployed, with no other income. Johann was responsible for big monthly payments plus a mountain of personal debt. Did I really want to sign up for this?

I used the sink to pull myself up off the floor, and was confronted with the sight of my ghostly white face and teary eyes in the mirror. I splashed cold water on my face, rinsed my mouth out with toothpaste, and regained my composure as best I could before walking back into the room.

"I need some time to process this," I said.

"I understand," he replied, his shoulders sagging under the weight of disappointment.

We picked at our dinner, making very little effort at conversation, then decided to go to bed.

It was a very long night. We lay there, side by side, silent, but still holding hands. Thoughts ricocheted inside my head. *We'll be in debt forever! How will we survive? Love is great, but you can't live on it! A smart person would just walk away, and I'm a smart person! But what if I never feel this way about anyone again?*

It was that last thought that scared me the most. I remembered a favourite quote: "Twenty years from now you will be more disappointed by the things that you didn't do than by the one you did do. So throw off the bowlines. Sail away from the safe harbour."

If I walked away from this wondrous, all-consuming feeling, I might regret it forever.

I decided to leave the safe harbour, knowing full well I may never return, with not a life raft, a flotation device or even a paddle in sight. I prepared myself for a long bout of sea sickness.

As first light crept in to the room, I rolled on to my side and propped myself up on my elbow to face Johann.

"You know, you've never formally proposed. If you really do want to marry me, you may want to do that."

"I will," he said, smiling, "when I find the perfect moment."

80

"Any time before the wedding will be fine."

We arranged the wedding over the internet. Although Johann was born and raised in South Africa, he'd never been to a game reserve or a bush lodge, so that became our choice of venue. It was a stretch for us financially, but I wanted our wedding to be special and memorable, so I agreed to foot the bill. Johann really struggled with this – he, too, wanted us to have a special wedding, but the fact that I was paying for it didn't sit well. From my perspective, if we were going to be in debt for the rest of our days, I at least wanted to have this to look back on.

The bride would be wearing black, as it was the only dress she had with her. The groom said he didn't mind, observing that nothing about this was traditional anyway.

After several hours of dull highway driving, the road curved and an entirely new landscape unfolded before us. We descended into lush green valleys and looked up at spectacular mountains. This was the Panorama Route, with some of the most remarkable scenery in what is arguably the most beautiful country on earth.

Following our downloaded instructions, we eventually reached the turnoff for the resort. We left the pavement and jostled down the dirt road for what seemed like an hour before we got to what turned out to be only the first gate.

We signed in with the security guard, who directed us down an even bumpier dirt road on the last leg of the trip. All discomfort was forgotten at the first sight of a majestic giraffe, grazing on a thorny umbrella tree.

Everything about these animals seems a contradiction. How can they be built so awkwardly yet move so gracefully? And how can they casually munch on thorns sharp enough to puncture the tires on your car? We sat and watched in wonder.

As we drove on, more bush residents came to greet us: blue wildebeest, kudu, zebra and impala. We were both thrilled.

It seemed like we'd been driving forever when we finally spied a small sign that read "Keep going. You are nearly there!"

As we pulled into the camp and parked next to the Mercedes and Land Rovers, I became acutely aware of the cracked windshield on our beaten-up borrowed car. I couldn't be sure, but I thought I saw the owner wince as he watched us pull up.

If he was in fact horrified, he hid it well as he greeted us warmly and offered us a drink. He showed us to our gorgeous out-of-a-travel-magazine "tent" – a concrete structure with a full en-suite bathroom as well as an outdoor shower at the back. The tent part was the canvas bedroom, which opened onto a private deck overlooking the dry riverbed and the watering hole where the animals would gather. It was all impressive, but what excited us most was the bed – double king size, I'm sure!

As soon as our escort had disappeared down the path, we launched onto the bed, laughing and jumping up and down. Johann took me in his arms and kissed me.

"You know, you still haven't asked me to marry you," I said.

"I'm waiting for the perfect moment."

"Well, I hope it happens tonight, because the wedding is tomorrow!"

We quickly changed into warmer clothes in preparation for our late-afternoon game drive. In this part of the country, the days are still hot in winter and this particular day was about 28 degrees. Overnight, though, the temperature can plummet to near freezing. We put on jeans, grabbed sweaters and jackets, and climbed onto the vehicle.

Sunset in the bush is a magical time. The animals who've been seeking shelter from the scorching sun emerge from their shady spots to enjoy the cooler air and head to the watering hole or out to look for dinner. As our vehicle moved along, we spied a head peering out of a deep dip in the road. As we approached, a lazy hyena stood up, yawned, stretched and moved to higher ground to pose for a photograph.

Then the real stars of the show appeared – two long, lean cheetahs, about to enjoy an unfortunate impala for dinner. We'd missed the chase and the kill. They'd caught the impala and were now catching their breath as they knelt on either side of the carcass, ready to dig in. We watched for a while, then set off to see who might have wandered down to enjoy the cool sand of the riverbed.

We were thrilled to find a pride of seven lions lounging in the twilight.

A question suddenly occurred to me. "Are you a cat person or a dog person?" I asked the man with whom I was going to spend the rest of my life.

"Definitely a cat person," he answered, much to my relief.

"Oh, good. Me too. We still have so much to learn about each other."

"Yes, and we have a whole lifetime to do it."

As the setting sun streaked the sky red and orange, our guide parked the Land Rover at the side of the road. He pulled out a picnic basket. Using the hood of the vehicle as a makeshift table, he set out snacks and poured a glass of red wine for each of us.

Surely this was the perfect moment? Johann put his arms around me and held me tight. "I love you, my lady," he said, but still he did not propose.

It was getting quite dark as we headed back to camp. Suddenly, two orange eyes shone bright in the headlights and a small leopard ambled past the vehicle. All the big cats in one drive – that had to be a good omen!

Johann was a bit flustered. "Did you see the way he looked at me?" he asked. "I think he had me in mind for his sundowner snack!"

When we returned to our tent, fluffy white terrycloth robes lay on the bed. It was time for our "bush bath". We slipped out of our clothes, donned the robes and were escorted down to a bathtub for two that was discreetly tucked in behind the cover of bushes and trees. The water was warm and smelled of lavender.

We lay there, looking up at the canopy of stars. This was it. This had to be the right moment. I looked expectantly into the eyes of my beloved and was surprised to see a look of … distress?

He leaned forward, took both my hands in his and said, "Jacquie Gauthier, will you marry me?"

"That's it? The perfect moment and that's your idea of a romantic proposal? Not even an 'I love you'?!" I spluttered.

"I'm sorry, love, but I'm completely thrown here. I've been waiting to ask you under Orion, just like that night in Sudan when I knew that I'd found the most special woman in the world. But I can't find Orion. He's not up there!"

If either of us had known a little more about astronomy,

we would have realized that in the southern hemisphere, Orion seldom gets above the horizon in the cold season. We'd met under a summer sky, but Johann was proposing in winter.

The next day we were up before the sun and heading out on our morning game drive. The lodge owner expressed his concern – did we really want to go? By the time we got back, we'd only have about half an hour to get ready for the wedding.

"That's okay," I said. "That's probably ten minutes more than I need." It was a bush wedding, after all, and I wasn't going to be a high-maintenance bride.

After spending the morning among the rhinos and giraffes, I quickly showered, and put on my black dress and a little makeup. The moment had come, and I was excited. I'd never felt so sure of anyone or anything in my entire life.

Our minister, a warm, round, outgoing man we affectionately nicknamed Friar Tuck, came to greet us. He asked if we were nervous.

"No," my groom said. "This just feels right."

The Friar introduced us to a gentleman who was learning to perform bush weddings and would act as his assistant. What a stroke of luck! We asked the assistant if he'd mind being the photographer as well, since we'd decided that was a luxury we couldn't afford. He readily agreed and started taking photos right away. He proved to be quite talented, so we do have some beautiful pictures of our wedding.

The minister escorted us to the game-drive vehicle, which had been freshly washed and decorated with palm fronds and branches from the magic guarri tree. We'd requested an African/Christian ceremony – the African for me, the Christian for Johann. In the tradition of the local Ndebele tribe, the women would use magic guarri branches to sweep the way for the bride, clearing away any bad luck. Of course, I had no bridesmaids to do the honours, so tying the branches to the vehicle would have to do the trick.

The pastor handed me my bouquet – cascading bush grasses surrounding three small pink impala lilies, which are the only flowers that bloom in winter here. They're said to bring happiness and prosperity. I prayed the lilies would work their magic for us, but it seemed a lot to ask from that trio of tiny blooms.

I was ready to get married. My dress was something old. The bouquet would have to qualify as something new. I wore the blue topaz earrings my parents had given me for Christmas years earlier. And the something borrowed was the ring I'd slip on the groom's finger.

Just prior to my trip, I'd gone to visit Grandma. She was in fact my ex-husband's grandmother, but we had formed a very close bond during my nine-year marriage to her grandson. I confided in her that I thought I had found the love of my life.

Intuitively feeling that the wedding would be sooner rather than later, she'd got up and gone into her bedroom, returning with the ring that had belonged to her late second husband – the love of *her* life, whom she hadn't found until she was well into her 70s. Never has there been a more charming man than "Mr Gordon" – as she still referred to him even after they were married. He was wise and witty, and when you walked into a room he always made you feel like you'd brought the sunshine with you.

When my marriage had ended, Grandma would always remind me to be patient, because my Mr Gordon was on his way.

She pressed his cherished wedding band into my hand and said, "I'm not quite ready to part with this yet, but I'd like you to take it with you, in case you need to use it."

After a short drive, we arrived at the scene where the ceremony would take place, a wooden platform nestled in the trees. It was an awkward climb up the small wooden ladder in my dress and kitten heels, but I made it with the help of a little push on the posterior from the groom. Johann, the minister and his assistant followed.

We all stood silently for a moment, taking in the view. The platform overlooked a watering hole. It made me smile to think that any animals who happened by for a drink would be our witnesses.

The ceremony was better than I could ever have imagined. The Friar seamlessly wove together stories from the

Bible with Ndebele tribal wisdom. We were given traditional gifts to give each other. Johann presented me with a blanket, boldly striped in vibrant hues of brown, gold, blue, red and green. It signified his intention to keep me safe, warm and protected.

I, in turn, gave him a small clay pot filled with beer to represent my promise to feed and care for him. Johann drank from the cup, and then offered some to me as a declaration of the equality in our relationship. The remainder of the beer was poured out on to the ground as an offering to the ancestors.

Before the exchange of vows, the minister produced a small branch from the buffalo-thorn tree. Tracing the curve of a thorn with his finger, he said, "The thorn is a hook. That curve represents your life up until now. It was the journey that brought you to where you're standing today. Now we're at the part where the thorn meets the branch. The branch symbolizes the life you have ahead of you, together.

"Before we go forward, I want you to take a moment to reflect on what you've brought with you from the past. If there's something that no longer serves you, now is the time to set it down and leave it behind, as you start out on this new journey together."

Could it be that simple? Could I just lay down my feelings of failure, disappointment and fear, and walk into happily-ever-after? It was certainly worth a try.

We exchanged our vows with traditional bracelets, Johann's made of copper, and mine a delicate brown, white, black and gold mosaic of beads. I then slipped Mr Gordon's treasured ring on Johann's finger. We were pronounced man and wife.

It was the beginning of our life together, but we had no idea where we'd live or how we could possibly make it work.

We climbed down off the platform and into the Land Rover to make our way back to the lodge. A tiny dwarf mongoose popped his head out of his hole and watched us go by. Then two zebras emerged from the bush and stood by the roadside.

"That's a good omen," said the Friar. "They're the perfect symbol for marriage. Their stripes are as unique as your fingerprints, but they live together in perfect harmony."

We got back to find champagne on ice and a small white frosted wedding cake decorated with fruit. We shared a toast with the minister and our photographer. Johann's hand was wrapped around mine as we cut the cake together. I felt a brief pang of regret that my family and friends weren't there to share in the celebration, but there was something very special about our intimate wedding.

And speaking of intimate, that moment would soon arrive. It wasn't that we'd been saving ourselves for marriage, but with the jet lag, the stress and the nerves, we hadn't yet managed to consummate our relationship. I wondered what it would be like. Our internet live chats sizzled, but how would it play out in person? The luxury safari tent was Harlequin Romance-worthy and I hoped our chemistry would be too.

But first, we had another chance to see the magnificent animals of the area. We hadn't even made it to the vehicle when the first elephant appeared – a big bull with long tusks came down to the waterhole for a drink. We stood on the deck watching him draw the water up through his trunk and splash it into his mouth. When he finished, he seemed to give us a nod before he slowly turned and walked away. I was elated.

"Elephants hold such a special place in my heart," I said, and told my new husband about my great-uncle and the little carving he'd given me. That gift had turned out to be the first of what grew to be an impressive herd of elephant carvings that I collected over the years. They occupied every room of my home. "In a way, I think elephants are what brought me to Africa."

"Then elephants have a special place in my heart, too," said Johann.

An entire herd met us as we pulled out of the lodge and we sat watching them feed for quite some time, feeling completely content in their peaceful presence.

By the time we got back from the drive, it was dark and the temperature had dropped dramatically. The ranger escorted us to our tent. We'd been warned to never walk alone after dark. We were in an open camp where the animals could come and go as they pleased. Only the elephants were kept out, by a single electric wire strung up about six feet off the ground. It was fine for leopards and lions to wander through camp at night, because they don't tend to do any damage. That wasn't the case with the elephants, however, and because the owner preferred having his tents and trees intact, the wire was in place to keep them at a safe distance.

We had about an hour before the ranger would come back and collect us for dinner. Despite the chill, we were excited about using the outdoor shower. It seemed like the perfect way to work up an appetite for what would come after dinner.

Johann quickly stripped off his jeans and sweater and went out to turn on the hot water. He stood there fiddling with the taps, trying to get the temperature just right. It was the first chance I'd had to really look at his naked body, and I liked what I saw. He was lean but muscular, especially across the chest and upper arms. His waist was slim, his stomach flat, and his butt compact and firm.

Then it was my turn. I undressed and turned to face the mirror. Would he be as impressed with my body as I was with his? Luckily, he didn't leave me much time to ponder that.

"Okay, love, come out! The water's fine," he called and I sprinted out to join him.

The steam from the warm water hitting the cold air enveloped us as he enveloped me. I was overwhelmed by all the incredible sensations: the warm water cascading down on me, his hard body pressing against me, his mouth hungrily exploring mine. I looked up at the stars and truly knew bliss. I closed my eyes, trying to capture this perfect moment forever in my mind.

Suddenly we were startled to hear footsteps approaching. We'd completely lost track of time! Johann grabbed a towel and wrapped it around his waist. He greeted the ranger at the entrance to the tent with "Hi, sorry, we'll be right with you."

We quickly dried off, dressed and emerged, grinning like idiots. The ranger gave us a knowing smile and led the way back to the lodge.

Our path was lit by the glow of lanterns and the lodge was bathed in the cozy orange-yellow light of candles and bonfires. Dinner was usually a communal affair where you shared the adventures of the day with the other guests, but this time we were escorted past the others in the main dining area down to a private deck overlooking the watering hole. An intimate table for two awaited us. Fire danced in the metal bowl set up next to the table to keep us warm. The flames made the silver and crystal on the table sparkle. Again I found myself trying to commit each detail of a perfect moment to my memory.

The crackling fire, the velvety red wine and the excitement warmed us as we enjoyed our meal. It seemed my senses were heightened. It was a feast for the eyes, the nose and the tongue. Fragrant warm chunks of homemade bread, peanut soup with ginger and coconut, tender lamb chops that all but melted in my mouth, and the perfect bittersweet balance of dark chocolate in the dessert. We savoured each bite and every moment. We looked up at the starry sky, and into each other's eyes.

The ranger escorted us back to our tent and bid us goodnight as he unzipped the flaps, revealing the room aglow with candles. Pink flower petals were strewn on the bed.

The moment had arrived.

My body tingled as Johann put his hand in the small of my back, drawing me closer to him. He kissed me tenderly, and I could feel the heat of desire rising in my body and his. In that moment the world outside, any fear, doubt or apprehension that lay in any part of my being, dissolved. I was ready to make love to my husband, my partner, my soul mate.

He slid his hands along my neck and pushed the dress back from my shoulders. As he undressed me, he kissed each part he uncovered, slowly working his way down until the dress fell to the floor. He picked me up, gently placing me on the bed, and held me like I was the most precious thing on earth.

We made love all night and greeted the dawn together. It was the first day of a new life for both of us.

What that life would look like and how it would work we had no idea, but none of that mattered in the moment. I knew that I had found my heart's desire.

7

Free State, South Africa

London and Penetanguishene, Canada

July to October 2010

It was time to face my new reality, and we set off back down the Panorama Route.

The scenery was spectacular as we left the Lowveld and started to ascend the mountain, traversing the pass and then gradually climbing higher to the part of the country called the Highveld. We could feel the shift in temperature with the change in altitude. Being Canadian, I hadn't expected to be cold in South Africa, but July is in the middle of winter, and where we were headed, Bloemfontein, the temperature often dropped below freezing at night.

Bloemfontein lies in the Free State, the breadbasket province of South Africa. We drove for over ten hours, leaving the mountains behind and passing through the flat fields that yield corn, wheat and sunflowers, and the pastures being grazed by large numbers of cattle and sheep.

Eventually, concrete buildings took shape in the distance and I knew we were close to the place my husband called home and where I would meet my new in-laws and my stepson. There was no telling how they'd react to the news of our wedding: they'd only recently been made aware of my existence, and now they would discover I was already part of their family.

Once again my nervous stomach was acting up. I was especially concerned about this first meeting with Johann's young son. Johann had said he was a very loving child, and wise beyond his 6 years, but I wondered how he'd feel about someone new in his father's life. I decided to take it slow, and wait for his cues to tell me how to proceed.

As we pulled up in front of Johann's parents' house, the door burst open. Johann barely had time to get out of the car before his son leapt into his arms, hugging him firmly with his entire body. Eventually, he slid back down to the ground, still clinging to his father's hand and retreating to hide behind his legs. Johann gently encouraged him to step forward so he could introduce us.

He took my hand and said a shy hello, barely glancing up from the ground. He quickly turned away, embracing his dad again and burying his face in Johann's legs.

By now my new in-laws had come out onto the front lawn. Johann introduced us, and they embraced me warmly.

We went inside the house and had tea. In a combination of Afrikaans and English, we talked about our trip and all the animals and sights we'd seen. The boy stayed close to his father, but I often found his eyes resting on me. When I smiled at him, he would shyly return the smile, then bury his face in Johann's lap.

Eventually, he went into his room, and returned with his favourite stuffed animal, a worn and obviously well loved grey rabbit named Wollie. He brought it over to me and placed it in my lap. I took that as a very good sign. I stroked the bunny's threadbare belly and gave it a hug. As the afternoon went on, the parade of toys continued, until I'd met them all.

Johann's sister and niece joined us for a family dinner. When the meal was finished, the boy slipped off his chair and headed to his room. A few minutes later, he peeked around the corner and crooked his finger, beckoning me to join him. Johann's eyes danced merrily as I excused myself from the table and was welcomed into his son's inner sanctum. He showed me all his books. I asked him to choose one and read it to him.

While I was exploring all the books and toys, Johann broke the news of our wedding to his family. They seemed genuinely pleased, and offered hugs and congratulations when I rejoined the group after story time.

We checked into a nearby guesthouse as there was no room for us with Johann's family. We were feeling relieved and content after the day's events.

Even though his son and I had hit it off, I still felt it was important that he and Johann have some time alone. The next morning I encouraged Johann to go on his own and spend the day reconnecting with his child. When he returned that evening, I asked how the day had gone.

"Great," he replied, "but he wanted to know why you didn't come. I said you thought that he and I might like some time alone, but he said he wants you to come, too."

The three of us spent the next few days together, playing in the park, going for walks and visiting the local zoo.

I left Bloemfontein feeling like a solid foundation had been laid for my relationship with my new family. There would be lots of time for us to get to know each other better later, but for now we were off to a good start.

Our brief honeymoon was soon over. We'd been married for less than a week when we found ourselves saying a sad goodbye at Johannesburg airport. I was returning to Canada, and I had no idea when I would see my husband again. Johann couldn't come with me because he had to apply for permanent-residence status in Canada, and we knew that process could take anywhere from six months to a few years. Since his Sudan contract had ended, he would be staying with his parents in their small home while he looked for work.

I desperately wanted to stay with him, but it wasn't possible.

"You have to go anyway, love." He tried to comfort me. "You have to sell your house and store your things. And you have to be there for your dad."

He was right. From a purely practical perspective, I had to wrap up all the details of my life. Then there was my dad, waiting to have major surgery to remove an aortic aneurysm. I wanted to be there for him, and to support my mom.

I also wanted to get the ball rolling on the immigration process that would allow Johann to come to Canada on a permanent basis. We were convinced that ultimately we'd be better off building a life on that side of the world, and that with Johann's international health-and-safety qualifications he'd be able to find a fulltime position and start building a career rather than going from contract to contract. I was anxious for him to find a job that didn't require him to live in a camp in the middle of nowhere with several hundred men where, for obvious reasons, wives were not welcome.

"You're right," I said, "but I hate leaving you, especially not knowing when I'll see you again."

"I promise you, it won't be long. By the time you get everything settled at your end, I'll have things organized at mine. I'll find a job somewhere, and we will be together."

When I got back to Canada, I set up an appointment with an immigration lawyer. We met for an hour, filling out the required forms to get the process in motion. As the meeting was drawing to a close, the lawyer said, "I hate to have to ask you this, but I really do need to know. Is Johann black or white?"

I was stunned by the question. "He's white," I replied, "but seriously, why on earth would you ask that question here in Canada, in this day and age? What difference can that possibly make?" I was absolutely incredulous.

"I know it's not right," he said, "but I have to be honest: the fact that he's white is about the only thing you have going for you. There are plenty of people who'd like to leave South Africa, and marrying a Canadian is an easy way to do it. I also need you to compile proof of your relationship – you know, things like photos, printouts of emails, and records of phone calls and text messages; also any letters from people who have met Johann and can vouch that this is a real relationship."

"They're going to read our emails? They're awfully personal, and to be honest a little... no, a lot risqué."

"Don't worry," the lawyer replied with a grin. "It's nothing the government officials haven't seen before and you can always black out those parts if you want to."

As I started to print out our emails, it became apparent that in some of them, the only thing not blacked out would be the date. I wrote to Johann and teased him about his penchant for using sexual innuendo and worse in his emails. "Could you just write a few I won't have to black out?" I asked.

"Nope," he replied in his next email. "It got me this far, so I'm not going to change now." He then proceeded to describe in great detail his plans for the first night that we'd finally be together again.

I finished gathering together all the "evidence" of our relationship and brought it down to the lawyer, who then submitted the application for Johann's permanent residence.

"Can he at least come for a visit while we wait for the outcome of this?" I asked.

"I really wouldn't advise it. If he applies for a visitors' visa and for some reason they turn him down, that will put a black mark on his file, and they may decide to deny the permanent residence application. It's not worth the risk."

There was nothing to do but wait.

Three months later, the deal on my house was about to close, and I started the enormous task of sorting through all my belongings. We had no idea where life would take us, so it was hard to know what to sell and what to keep. I tried to be ruthless, except when it came to art and other sentimental things. In the end, after a big yard sale, I had a manageable number of boxes and pieces of furniture left, and I had them moved north to store in my parents' basement until we knew where we were going to live. I planned to stay with my folks until my dad had had his surgery and was well on the road to recovery.

About a month later, Dad was admitted to the hospital. My mother and I spent several anxious hours in the waiting room while they were operating. Then we received two pieces of good news: a nurse came in to say that Dad was fine and resting in the recovery room; then I got a text message from my husband telling me that he had a job. "We're moving to Kroonstad in the Free State," the text read.

I quickly typed my reply: "I don't know where that is, but okay! I'll be there as soon as I can!"

Within a week, I was on my way back to South Africa. In my bag I carried two elegant white-gold wedding bands. My friends had all contributed to the project, rounding up their broken gold chains and stray earrings, which were melted down by another friend, a talented jeweller. With the scrap gold he was able to produce replicas of Grandma and Mr Gordon's wedding rings. Both rings were inscribed with lyrics taken from one of Johann's and my favourite love songs, "History in the Making" by Darius Rucker. Written inside Johann's ring is "Last first kiss". Engraved inside mine is "A chance worth taking".

I couldn't wait to slip the ring on his finger and really, finally begin our life together. We'd been apart for three months, and I couldn't wait to see my husband again.

This time, as the plane began its decent into Johannesburg, I was nothing but excited. Johann was there waiting for me at the gate when I got through customs. I literally jumped into his arms.

It was already quite late, and I'd been in transit for over a day, so we'd booked a hotel near the airport for the night. Kroonstad was about a two-hour drive away; it would wait until the next morning.

When we got to our room, I produced the ring box from my bag. We reminisced about the wedding and said our own version of vows as we slipped the sparkling rings on each other's fingers. We fell asleep intertwined, and I slept better than I had in months.

We awoke early the next morning and I was excited to drive to our new city and see the place that would be our first marital home. I had no idea what to expect. Johann had written to me that he'd found a little flat in Kroonstad that we could afford. He'd said it was in a nice neighbourhood, and that I'd be able to walk to a few shops, but he really hadn't said too much more about it.

I was about to find out why he'd chosen to keep the details to himself.

8

Kroonstad, Free State, South Africa

November 2010

Beep, beep, beep.

The insistent sound of Johann's watch alarm signalled the awful truth. It was 6 o'clock and the dawn of a new day in Kroonstad, Free State, South Africa.

But was it Wednesday? Maybe Friday?

The sleeping pill hadn't worn off yet, so my foggy mind couldn't figure it out. Not that it mattered anyway. Each day was a depressing duplicate of the one before. The only exception was Sunday, which was worse than the other days because the whole place shut down. There's a standing joke that you should never go skydiving in Kroonstad on a Sunday because nothing will open.

Johann rolled over and put his arm around me, drawing my head on to his chest. We lay like this for a few minutes and I tried to focus on the soothing rhythm of his heartbeat and the warmth of his body against mine. I wished we could stay like this all day, but a gentle kiss on my forehead told me it was time to get on with our morning routine.

I reluctantly released him and he headed for the shower. I got up and took the four steps required to get from the bed to the kitchen counter. I pressed the coffee maker's red button and it gurgled to life, sputtering water into the filter. It seemed to struggle as much as I did in the morning but soon the glorious brown liquid trickled through and began to pool at the bottom of the pot. Filter coffee was one of the few luxuries we allowed ourselves.

Most people here drank something instant that's a blend of coffee, chicory and God knows what else. It was affordable but it wasn't coffee. The longlife milk they nearly half-filled the mug with was also suspect – what did they do to it so that it could sit on the shelf for months without refrigeration? And to mask the taste of the coffee and the alleged milk, most put in three to four heaping teaspoons of sugar.

I went back into the bedroom and opened the cupboard to lay out Johann's clothes – briefs, undershirt, socks and the navy-blue flight suit that served as his paramedic uniform, and his black safety boots.

The bathroom's accordion door unfolded, revealing my now clean and clean-shaven husband. He poured two mugs of coffee and brought them into the bedroom. I crawled back under the covers and propped my pillow against the wall to use as a back rest.

I watched him dress. We didn't talk much because there wasn't much to say. He had to go and I didn't want him to.

Johann packed his orange knapsack with the essentials: his phone and laptop, a plastic container with last night's leftovers, and a couple of apples.

Next came the hard part. We kissed goodbye and I walked outside to unlock and open the gate while he got into the car. He reversed the car through the gate, stopping for a moment to mouth "I love you" before turning on to the street and driving off for his ambulance shift.

Now my job began: finding ways to occupy my body and my mind for the next thirteen hours.

When I worked in radio, we used a process known as back timing. You started with the time you wanted to finish, then added the elements that would fill the time until you worked your way back to the time you'd started. I applied the system to the day ahead of me.

Johann would get home at about 7.30pm. That meant I could start dinner preparations at 6 o'clock. We had a bit of leftover chicken and some carrots, radishes and onions from the garden, so I could make a stir-fry. I liked that idea because all the chopping would take a while.

At 5 o'clock I could start getting myself ready. I could take a long shower, do my hair, put on some makeup and dress up a bit. In my early-morning radio-host days, I could get all those things done in less than half an hour. I hadn't been able to stand the thought of setting my alarm for any earlier than half past three in the morning, but I still had to be ready to leave the house by 4am, so I'd learned to move fast. Now, with a concerted effort, I could manage to draw out the process to fill an entire hour.

Oprah would be on at 4 o'clock in the afternoon, so that would kill an hour.

That left eight hours to fill. If the sleeping pill hadn't quite worn off, there was a chance I could go back to sleep and shave another hour off that, and so only have seven hours left. Some days I was lucky and I did manage to get back to sleep but I'd become a complete insomniac since moving to Kroonstad.

When I thought about how to describe my new life, the word "deprived" seemed to sum it up best. I felt deprived of sleep, money, communication, company and stimulation. I felt deprived of a sense of security and of wellbeing.

The only thing I was not lacking was love. That was the decision I'd made: to trade everything for love. I had always believed that love conquered all. I hoped to be proven right.

I woke for the second time that morning just after 8 o'clock. I popped in my trusty DVD and assumed the required yoga poses until 9 o'clock. I showered, put on shorts and a T-shirt, and ventured out beyond the big iron gates that protected and imprisoned us.

Our first marital home was a dreary cottage tucked in behind our landlord's house. He'd left a larger city to come back to his hometown of Kroonstad, which he told me daily had been a big mistake.

"You'll go crazy in this one-horse town," he said.

I was afraid he might be right. From the time I arrived in Kroonstad, I started losing my voice. At first I didn't know if it was the hot dry weather or the jet lag. After a while, I thought it might be due to the fact that I would go for hours on end without uttering a word but then I started to worry that it might be a physical reflection of my emotional state. Maybe crazy was just around the corner.

Distressingly, my one bit of daily social interaction was with the landlord. He'd bought the house when he retired from his job as a tobacco company executive several years earlier; he'd told me candidly that he'd chosen early retirement after the 1994 election which put an end to apartheid – he didn't think he'd be able to handle the changes integration would bring to his workplace.

He had a lush front garden – a truly beautiful green oasis with flowers, herbs and a pond stocked with brightly coloured koi fish. Based on that first impression, I'd expected to walk in his front door and see a beautifully appointed home. I couldn't have been more wrong. There was all manner of stuff strewn from the front entrance all the way to the back door. His entire home was his workshop – he fancied himself quite a handyman, taking on any and all projects, all at the same time. Nothing ever seemed to get finished, and each day a new

109

project or repair took precedence over the one started the day before.

Even the entire house wasn't big enough to accommodate all the stuff, so it had spilled out the rear door and completely taken over the back yard. To get to the clothesline, I'd have to navigate an obstacle course of plumbing and electrical parts, scrap metal, broken glass and other assorted junk.

I wanted to take pictures of the scene because I didn't think anyone would believe me when I described it. Johann begged me not to; in fact, he asked me not to tell my family and friends about it because he felt so embarrassed that this was how we were living.

"What did you do for a living when you were in Canada?" the landlord asked as we were gathering herbs in the front garden one morning.

"I was a radio personality. I did a morning show."

He thought for a moment then said, "So, you went from talking to everyone, to no one to talk to."

For all the talking I used to do, I couldn't have said it better.

Language turned out to be a bigger barrier than I'd expected. If we'd moved to a larger centre, English would have been more prevalent, but I would've had even less social interaction, because we likely wouldn't have been able to afford a place in a neighbourhood where it would have been safe for me to walk around alone. With so many people financially desperate, the crime rate in South Africa is extremely high. Even in this relatively small city, we lived behind a locked gate with bars on our windows. Homes were gated and surrounded with barbed wire, and many had vicious dogs in the yard.

I never knew loneliness the way I knew it in Kroonstad. There were days I thought I'd lose my mind. You can only do so much yoga and watch so much *Oprah*.

I found my surroundings overwhelmingly depressing. The cottage was small and dingy. No amount of scrubbing could remove the grey cast from the white floors. There's an ill wind that blows through Kroonstad. Okay, maybe that's a bit dramatic, but there seemed to be an ever-present wind that blew dirt into the house. At first I swept several times a day. Soon I stopped caring, and eventually I stopped noticing.

Our scavenged mismatched furniture was harder to ignore. We had a burgundy chair and a love seat that were both ugly and uncomfortable. As an added bonus, the love seat smelled of stale cat urine which defied every odour-masking product on the market. I washed it with laundry detergent, dishwashing liquid and baking soda. I sprayed it with antibacterials and air fresheners. The rancid smell still hung in the air. If I had to live with the smell, I wished I at least had the company of the cat.

Then one day a cat walked into my life, slipping through the bars of the open kitchen window. I'd seen him in the yard a few times and had tried to get friendly with him, but the landlord didn't care for cats, and would always chase him away. The clever black-and-white kitty eventually figured out how to circumvent the landlord by going around to the back of the cottage and entering through the window.

He didn't have a collar, so I didn't know his name or if he had an owner. I named him Jack.

Jack's visits became frequent, sometimes six a day. He'd come in through the window and launch himself over the sink, signalling his presence with the soft thump of his front paws as he jumped from the countertop to the floor. He'd casually stride into the lounge like he owned the place, then rub up against my leg and plop down on his back, purring, expecting a belly rub.

During his first visit of the day, as I gave him the affection he demanded, I'd check him for injuries from the night before. Jack was a real scrapper and seemed to need to defend his supremacy over the neighbourhood on an almost nightly basis. Scratches and missing tufts of fur were common.

One day he appeared with his eye sewn shut. Fortunately, some kind soul had taken the injured warrior to a vet – or maybe he did have an owner, after all. I hoped that when the stitches were removed, his eye would be functional. Sadly, it wasn't – so I changed his name to One-Eyed Jack.

For better or for worse, that ordeal didn't change his personality. He remained incredibly affectionate with me but continued to roam the streets at night, picking fights with any cat that dared to challenge him.

While Jack provided me with companionship and much-needed distraction, it wasn't enough. I still needed to get out.

There were two excursions I could make that were deemed safe for me to tackle on my own. One was my daily fifteen-minute walk to the grocery store, and the other the five-minute walk to the marshland just behind our place. After Johann had left for work, I'd go there and sit under the magnificent eucalyptus tree, observing the cheerful red bishops nesting in the tall grass.

A few hours later, I'd take my daily walk to the grocery store. In typical Canadian fashion, I greeted everyone I met en route. I came to view this as a social experiment. The reaction was invariably one of surprise, but for different reasons, depending on which race I approached. The whites looked at me like I was crazy; their expression seemed to say, "I don't know you; why are you talking to me?" The blacks appeared surprised that I'd acknowledged them, but would quickly recover and reward me with a genuine smile or a "Good day, ma'am".

One day, when I was feeling particularly lonely, I went out for a second afternoon stroll along my all-too-familiar route. A full-figured black woman wearing a vibrant fuchsia dress approached.

As we were just about to pass each other, I impulsively reached out and touched her arm. "That colour looks beautiful on you," I said.

She giggled with pleasure and replied, "Thank you."

We both walked away with a little more spring in our step, and I marvelled at what a big difference a small gesture can make.

All races bear the scars of living in a culture of distrust and fear. The political changes since 1994 have barely patched the surface of this social chasm that may never heal. Racism in all forms still runs deep. Every day I'd hear things said that offended my North American ears and sensibilities. These statements were sometimes prefaced with, "I'm not being racist, but..." Other times, there was no attempt to hide the contempt.

Johann's boss at the ambulance service was one of the worst offenders. One Saturday afternoon, when Johann and I were walking to the grocery store, we saw him at the wheel of the ambulance in the parking lot. My instinct was to turn and walk the other way, because I really didn't like the man, but Johann insisted that it would be rude not to go over and say hello.

As we approached the vehicle, we were surprised to see he had a large snake in his hands. I was completely shocked. "Gee, what are you trying to do?" I asked. "Give your patients a heart attack if they haven't had one already?"

"He's my new pet," he responded. "I'm going to start breeding these snakes to sell them. They're worth a lot of money."

Just then a couple of black men approached the vehicle. They were curious to see the creature and had slowed down to have a look.

"Don't worry," the boss said. "Come closer; he won't bite you."

The pair moved a little closer, and just as they got up to the window, he thrust the snake at them while making a loud noise to make sure he scared them half to death.

"Sorry, my friends," he said, laughing. "I forgot snakes don't like black people."

They turned and started to walk away, shaken and humiliated.

I was furious.

"Wait!" I called. "Please don't listen to him. That's just not true. He's the one who should worry. Snakes don't like morons."

On another hot sunny Saturday, while Johann was at work, the landlord invited me to go to the monthly fleamarket downtown. Of course, I jumped at the chance. Visions of a used-book stall danced in my head.

"It's not much," he said, "but at least it's something to do for a change."

As we drove downtown, we were forced to stop to give way to a group of teenagers who were sauntering unhurriedly across the road.

"See how they walk," the landlord fumed. "I hate the blacks."

We carried on to the fleamarket, but the outing had lost its lustre for me.

I did find a stall selling secondhand books where I picked up a copy of James A Michener's epic 1980 history of South Africa, *The Covenant*. I hoped reading it would help me better understand the bitterness and hatred still carried in the hearts of so many to this day.

As far as excitement goes, the monthly fleamarket was about it for Kroonstad. We didn't choose the town because it was a great place to live. It was really just a case of economic survival. As a paramedic for a private company, Johann only made the equivalent of about $1,000 a month. That salary was across the board, whether you worked in a city like Pretoria that has a high cost of living or in a smaller centre where your rand would stretch further.

Rent in Kroonstad was relatively affordable, eating up about a third of our income. Johann's financial obligations from his previous marriage took up the rest, and more. He had to work overtime shifts to pay for fuel, food, telephone and internet.

The limited airtime we bought was used up by the online health-and-safety courses Johann was taking to try to get a better job. I only went online a couple of times a week to check email. I'd write my responses offline, and a few times a week, log on to quickly cut, paste and send them off using minimal data.

We were trying hard to live on Johann's income. My hands were tied because I was in the country on a relatives' permit, which required me to submit a written job offer to be able to apply for a work permit. The only way an employer could offer me a job was to advertise the position nationally and have no qualified South African apply. Unfortunately, my broadcasting talents didn't transfer well to this part of the world, so the chances of an employer jumping through the bureaucratic hoops required to hire me seemed highly unlikely.

My savings in Canada were dwindling fast. I'd used a big chunk to pay off some of Johann's debt, which turned out to be throwing good money after bad. We ended up being unable to keep up with all the payments and the creditors were calling nearly every day. We'd defaulted on the car loan, so it was about to be repossessed.

While we never missed a support payment for Johann's son, we couldn't possibly meet the court-ordered alimony payments to his former wife. She, too, called almost daily, trying to get blood from a stone.

This was all so foreign to me. My dad had taught me well where money was concerned. I'd never been in debt in my life, and now I felt like I was drowning in it.

I became more and more depressed and felt completely isolated. I spent most mornings crying, and the afternoons trying to pull myself together, make dinner and seem normal by the time Johann got home. I didn't want my husband to know just how close I was to coming completely unglued. I was afraid I was going to have a nervous breakdown.

He beat me to it.

The stress of the situation completely overwhelmed him one day at work, and Johann broke down, sobbing in the back of the ambulance. As much as I'd tried to hide my emotional state, he was of course acutely aware of it, and he blamed himself. He felt he was failing as a husband, a father and a provider. He'd crossed the line between depression and despair.

Luckily, the hospital where the ambulance service was based had a mental-health programme called Time Out. Johann was assessed by one of the doctors and was diagnosed with post-traumatic stress disorder brought on by a number of factors over the years, including the time he'd spent in Sudan. He was to be admitted into the Time Out programme, where he'd receive therapy daily for two weeks. That meant I would only be able to see him for one hour each evening.

I resolved to pull myself together and support him through the process.

The first day passed slowly, and I could hardly wait until 7 o'clock when I could go for my visit. I felt a flood of relief when I saw him sitting up in his hospital bed, reading. He looked relaxed, and his face lit up when he saw me in the doorway.

It had been a good first day. He told me about the session with his psychologist and the group session with the psychiatrist that followed.

"I'm really enjoying this book you gave me," he said, indicating the copy of Paulo Coelho's *The Alchemist* that lay on his lap.

We were both feeling quite optimistic by the time the nurse came to usher me out at the end of the visit.

The next day, once again, I spent the entire day anticipating our evening visit. At 6:30 I started my leisurely walk to the hospital. At precisely 7 o'clock, I walked past the nurses' station on the way to Johann's room.

One of the nurses called to me, and asked me to join her in an empty examination room.

"I have some bad news," she said. "Your medical insurance has rejected Johann's claim. He will have to leave the programme tomorrow."

"How can that be? They must have approved the claim otherwise he wouldn't have been admitted."

119

"They've changed their minds," she said.

"Can they do that?" I asked incredulously.

"They did," she replied. "Johann has to leave after his session tomorrow, and to make matters worse, now we have to charge you for the two days he's already been in here."

Before I even got to his bedside, Johann could see that I'd heard the news.

"It'll be okay, love. My psychologist is pretty upset about this, and she's agreed to continue seeing me as an outpatient. We'll work out the payments with her."

"That's great," I said. "And we won't worry about the money. I'll sell some of my furniture in Canada, or my family will help us. All that's important now is that you get well."

He came home the next day, and while I was still worried about him, it was a relief to have him back. We decided to do whatever we could to lessen our stress. We sought help from a debt counsellor and went into a programme that would stop the phone calls from the creditors; that alone was a tremendous relief. Johann filed papers with the court to reassess his alimony payments in light of our circumstances. His ex-wife had found a good job and was making more money than he was, so the alimony was dropped, leaving only the child-support payments.

We then made a conscious decision to do whatever we could to increase our joy. We made a practice of noticing, appreciating and enjoying every good thing in each day. We'd go for walks, pointing out and admiring the clouds in the sky, the leaves on the trees, the vibrant colours of the flowers, and the intricate combinations of colours and patterns on the wings of the butterflies.

Johann went back to work. Over the following weeks, he made remarkable progress. It was good to see him smile again.

One morning he woke me early, bringing me a cup of coffee in bed.

"Get dressed and grab your camera," he said. "There's something I want to show you."

Our car had been repossessed, so he'd borrowed a car from a friend. I tried to enjoy the drive, but I was very conscious of the high price of fuel. The further we got from town, the more anxious I became about the money this was costing.

"Where are you taking me?"

"Relax," he said. "It's a surprise."

And what a beautiful surprise it was! Gorgeous, enormous sunflowers, as far as the eye could see – fields on fields of them.

"I love sunflowers!" I exclaimed.

"I know you do," he said. "When we've seen the odd one at the side of the road, you've always said they're the most cheerful flower there is. I drove past these fields on an ambulance call the other day, and I knew I had to bring you here on my next day off. Now, grab your camera and go take some wonderful photos."

With that, he prized apart two strands of the wire fence so I could crouch down and crawl through. As I walked among the vibrant yellow flowers, I couldn't stop grinning. I looked back at my husband and saw he was doing the same.

9

Kroonstad

December 2010

Is there a devil? Does this wicked creature walk among us?

I'd always doubted the existence of this being, but apparently it does exist, and I was quite surprised to learn that it was me!

Johann's ex-wife had come to this conclusion for two reasons. One was that we'd married so quickly. In her mind, no one would ever do that, so obviously Johann and I had been carrying on a torrid affair while they'd still been married. How we would ever have pulled that off I'm not sure, but perhaps that's one of the advantages of being Satan – you aren't hindered by the minor constraints of space and time.

The second reason was that I had no children. This was, apparently, at best a serious character flaw; at worst, it renders you a complete freak of nature.

I admit I was never one of those girls who always knew her aspirations lay in marriage and motherhood. I hadn't ruled it out, but I didn't have that burning desire that so many of my friends seemed to have. If I examine my late childhood and teenage years, I guess it's easy to see why.

When I was 9 years old, my younger sister arrived. Then, two years after that, my parents welcomed another daughter, but sadly she wasn't a healthy baby. A genetic defect meant that she'd never grow and develop normally; and then there was the matter of the hole in her heart. The doctors didn't think she'd ever leave the hospital, but her little soul had other plans, and she stayed with us for five years.

My mother already had more than she could handle, with a toddler and a babe in arms, when my grandfather came to live with us. He'd had a stroke, which left him paralyzed on his left side and completely unable to speak.

The burden of care was enormous, and my elder sister and I were Mother's little helpers. I guess that by the time my sister died and my grandfather had to be moved to a nursing home, I felt I'd fulfilled my role as caregiver for this lifetime.

That's not to say I didn't ever consider having a family. There was a three-month period during my previous marriage when the idea was seriously discussed and considered. Admittedly, at the time, it had seemed pretty appealing, but deep down I think I knew the marriage was in trouble, and having a baby to make things better is rarely a good idea.

I had actually started to feel quite guilty about my choice when an acquaintance remarked that it's selfish not to want to have children. I found that deeply troubling. Was I being selfish? I discussed it with my mother, who made the very astute observation that it's selfish either way: you have children because you want to, or you don't because you don't.

It had been five months since my first meeting with my stepson, and he was due to come from Johannesburg and stay with us for the week leading up to Christmas. Johann was over-the-moon excited, but I was apprehensive. Whenever his ex-wife spoke to Johann on the phone, which was nearly every day, I'd hear her loud and angry voice. She was Afrikaans, so I never knew exactly what she was saying, but the word *slet* sounds remarkably similar to its English equivalent, so I definitely caught the drift of the conversation. Because of her obvious hostility toward me, I worried that my stepson may have been subjected to a negative PR campaign against me.

My concern turned out to be valid. Everything had changed since the last time we'd seen each other. Literally from the moment he arrived, his altered attitude was obvious. I'd gone from being his friend, to the woman who lives with his father. In his new view, I was nothing to him, and my role was to look after him when his dad was at work.

It was going to be a very long week.

Early the next day, we waved goodbye as Johann pulled out of the driveway, on his way to the ambulance base at the hospital for his shift. It would be thirteen hours until he came home for dinner. There was nothing to do but make the most of the situation, and hope for the best.

"C'mon," I said, "let's draw something. I've got crayons and some paper for you."

"No thanks," he said. "I don't like to draw."

"Well, that's not what I hear," I replied. "I hear you love it, and that you're really good at it."

"Okay," he said grudgingly.

We sat down at the table and both took paper and crayons. He stared at the blank page for a few seconds. "I don't know what to draw," he said.

"Well, how about a race car?"

"Okay."

About three minutes later he handed me the paper.

"I'm done. This is boring. Let's watch a movie."

"Well, we watched a movie last night, and I promise you can watch one tonight before bed, but it's a really nice day. Let's go for a walk to the marsh to see the red bishops."

"What's a red bishop?" he asked.

"Come with me and you'll see," I replied.

We hadn't even made it to the end of the block when the complaints started.

"It's too hot."

126

"Yes, I know it's warm, but it's still early, and it's going to get a lot worse, so that's why we're going now. Otherwise, we'll be inside all day."

"How much further?" he asked.

"Two more blocks," I replied.

I made a few attempts at conversation, pointing out the flowers, the birds and the trees along our route, but he'd chosen the silent treatment as his strategy.

Finally, we got to the marsh. It was a spectacular sight, with hundreds of small red-and-black birds flying through the air and perched on the reeds.

He was so impressed that he momentarily forgot his vow of silence.

"Wow!"

"Yeah, they're pretty wow, aren't they?"

That magical moment was shortlived.

"Now what are we going to do?" he demanded.

"Ah, let's see. There's a swing over there – I'll race you to it!"

I took off immediately, with him in hot pursuit. As we approached the swing, I slowed my pace and he zoomed past.

"I won!" he said smugly.

"You sure did."

"Push me," he said as he hopped up on the swing.

"I'd be happy to, if you ask nicely."

"Okay. Please," he said.

Again after a few short minutes, the thrill was gone. He jumped off the swing, and raced over to a big eucalyptus tree. He tried to climb it but couldn't get a foothold.

"Boost me up," he demanded.

"No, I think that's a bad idea. If I get you up into that first branch, you'll be pretty high up, and you might get scared. You may not be able to climb down, and I won't be able to reach you."

"I won't get scared. Boost me up! Pleeeease!"

"It's not a good idea."

"Pull-eeeeeease!"

"Fine," I said, ignoring my better judgment. I grabbed him under the arms and lifted him as high as I could.

He held on to the trunk and put his feet on my shoulders. He grasped the lowest branch, then became completely panic stricken.

"It's too high! I'm scared!" he wailed.

At this point an "I told you so" would've been sweet, but clearly wasn't appropriate. Now I had to figure out how to get him back down without injuring us both.

"Okay, calm down," I said. "I'll get you down."

He cried and screamed louder.

"Please, calm down. You can get back down exactly how you got up. Let go of the branch, grab the trunk, and stand on my shoulders."

By now, he was crying hysterically and kicking madly.

"Please," I begged. "Stop! Take a deep breath and calm down or we're both going to get hurt."

I got a hard kick to the clavicle from his flailing feet as he tried to find my shoulders. I raised my arms and grabbed his waist to steady him as he hugged the tree trunk, and we slid down to the ground, landing in a tangled heap.

He immediately jumped up and took off.

"I'll race you to that big tree!" he called over his shoulder.

I pulled myself up off the ground and walked over to meet him at the tree.

"We need to talk about what just happened," I said. "When I tell you something is a bad idea, it's because I'm looking out for you. You got very scared, you kicked me hard, and you're very lucky you didn't get hurt. Understand?"

"Can we go home now?" he asked.

It was only half past nine. Three hours down, ten to go.

When Johann finally got home around half past seven that evening, his boy's demeanour changed entirely. He was talkative, outgoing and affectionate with his dad, while ignoring me completely. This made Johann feel terrible, so he kept trying to include me in conversations and being very affectionate with both of us.

I felt badly for him. I knew how happy it would make him if we could be like a family, but that would have to come in its own time and in its own way. Or maybe not at all. The only thing I knew for sure was that forcing things would make matters worse.

It was frustrating and painful for Johann to feel caught in the middle between two people he loved so much. One of the most endearing things about my husband is his desire to make everyone happy.

As is quite common behaviour among children of divorce, his son pressed things to his full advantage. If I said he couldn't have potato chips for breakfast, he would go to his father, who would allow him a small bowl.

One morning I went out for a walk on my own and came

home to discover that the chicken I'd earmarked for dinner that night had been eaten for a midmorning snack. I was really upset. Our budget was beyond tight, and I had to plan every meal to make the most of what we had.

It was this sort of thing that caused real friction between Johann and me.

"I know you don't see him often and you don't want to be the bad guy, but he doesn't respect me, and all you're doing is confirming that he doesn't have to listen to me," I pointed out to Johann. "If you're going to put me in a position where I have to look after him, then you have to support me when I lay down rules."

Later that evening, as Johann prepared to leave us for an overnight shift, he sat his son on his knee and gave clear instructions. "You can watch a movie until 8 o'clock. Then you must put on your pajamas and brush your teeth and get into bed. After that, you can watch something until 9, but then it's lights out and you must go to sleep."

His son nodded his agreement.

Once his dad was gone, he chose a movie and I popped it into the DVD player. When 8 o'clock rolled around, I pressed pause and said, "Okay, it's time to put on your pajamas and brush your teeth, then you can watch the rest in bed."

"No," he said, folding his arms across his chest defiantly.

I tried to reason with him. "You promised your dad that you would. Now you have to live up to your promise."

He didn't bother to respond and continued to stare me down. I crossed my arms in response, and returned his stare. My outward calm masked my internal turmoil. *Great,* I thought, *now what do I do? I can't back down but what if this goes on for hours?*

After several minutes that seemed like an eternity, I decided to say something.

"I don't know about you," I ventured, "but I'd much rather be watching the end of the movie than sitting here like this for hours."

He apparently saw the wisdom in this, as his defiance was already becoming boring. Without comment, he uncrossed his arms, slid off the couch and went into the bathroom to brush his teeth.

And so it went for the rest of the week. I felt I was constantly being tested. I tried to stay calm and consistent in my approach, but it just wasn't working. Nothing was about to make him change his mind about me.

When it came time for his father to drive him back to his mother in Johannesburg, he walked out the door without so much as a goodbye. Embarrassed, Johann told him to come back and say goodbye and thank you. He did so but less than half-heartedly.

I was so shaken up by the visit that I made an appointment with Johann's therapist to try to figure out what had gone so drastically wrong.

"I'm not his mother, nor do I want to be, but if he's going to be in my care, I have to do what I think is right," I confided to the therapist. "I didn't think it was right to let him sit in front of the TV all day. And I thought if we did some things together, it would help us to get past all the hostility and he'd remember that he liked me when we first met."

"There's nothing wrong with what you did; you just didn't get the result you were hoping for," she observed. "All you can do is your best. How he responds is completely out of your control."

I can only hope that with the passage of time my stepson and I will be able to forge a better relationship. Maybe some day he'll think of me as his "wicked-awesome" stepmom.

10

Mabula Lodge, Limpopo, South Africa

March 2011

Obviously, our life in Kroonstad wasn't the experience of Africa I'd hoped for. I longed to spend more time in the bush.

Through a friend in Canada, I sold some of my jewellery and was able to pay my tuition to enrol at the Limpopo Field Guide Academy. If I was up to the task, I'd come out of the bush in three weeks with a qualification that would allow me to work guiding tourists at a lodge, once I had my permanent residence.

It took five hours to drive from Kroonstad to Mabula Private Game Reserve in the Waterberg region of Limpopo province. As soon as we arrived, Johann unloaded my luggage, kissed me goodbye, and started the long drive back home.

I felt a wave of anxiety as I watched him drive away. I hadn't been in school for almost three decades and I had no experience in the bush. Could I really do this?

I was shown to the room I'd share with the only other woman taking the course. There were to be sixteen of us all together – fourteen men, mostly Afrikaners, and two women, both of us foreigners. I wondered how we'd be received.

My roommate still hadn't arrived, so I chose the bed closest to the door and started to unpack and settle in.

Suddenly, Hurricane Bea blew in. She was a tall wiry woman with big brown eyes, long dark hair and a thick Italian accent.

Bea dumped her belongings on the other bed and went into the bathroom to use the toilet, talking all the while and not bothering to close the door. It was already clear that boundaries and modesty would not apply for the next three weeks.

"Ah, this is wonderful, no? Very exciting. I hope you are okay sharing a room with me. Most women don't like me."

I was rescued from this conversation by a knock on the door. It was Shani, one of the instructors, telling us to make our way to the boma, the walled outdoor area that would serve as our kitchen, dining room and study hall for the next few weeks.

Once the group had assembled, we were quickly divided into two teams and led to an obstacle course. This definitely hadn't been in the brochure – nor was it in my comfort zone!

The first component of the course required crawling on gravel under barbed wire. I instantly regretted my wardrobe choice – shorts and a tank top. When one of the guys finished

135

his turn, I quickly commandeered his long-sleeved shirt to protect my arms and elbows. There was nothing to be done about my legs and knees, which emerged scraped and bloody.

Next came the task of walking across the high beam. I'm very afraid of heights, but I managed to make it through by making jokes and calling on members of both teams for assistance.

This became my strategy for the rest of the challenge – to make people laugh, and ask for help. It turned out that this actually worked in my favour – unbeknown to us, we were being assessed not on our physical abilities, but on our attitude and ability to be part of a team.

The days started just before dawn. We were paired into work teams – my roommate was also my workmate, which meant we were pretty much joined at the hip all day, every day. Duties rotated between checking and preparing the Land Rovers for the game drives, meal preparation and general camp duties. All other waking hours were consumed with game drives, lectures, assignments and study time.

To say this was a crash course in nature guiding is an understatement. The sheer volume of information we had to absorb was overwhelming, especially for a foreigner who was completely unfamiliar with the local flora and fauna. (Since I did the course, the three-week programme has been expanded to three months, which is far more appropriate.)

For our first oral presentation, we were each to give a report about a tree. We had to research its practical uses, medicinal uses and any associated tribal folklore. And we had to find an example of that tree while out on a game drive. This worried me, as tree identification was not proving to be my strong suit. It can be tricky and often a young tree doesn't look like its mature version.

Much to my relief, I was assigned the tamboti tree, easily identified by its dark, block-patterned bark. At least I should have no trouble finding one in the bush when it came time for me to give my presentation.

When the day came, I felt completely prepared and we hadn't been driving for long when I spotted a beautiful specimen of my tree. I pointed it out and asked the driver to stop. We all climbed out of the vehicle and assembled around its impressive trunk.

As I started to explain the uses for the poisonous milky latex produced in the bark, Bea casually took two steps back, dropped her shorts and proceeded to relieve herself.

The guys in the class were for once rendered speechless. I was literally sinking my teeth into my tongue to stop myself from laughing.

I regained my composure and carried on, knowing that from then on, the stately tamboti would always be known to me as the Bea-pee tree.

In addition to learning some botany, I had to become well versed in animal identification and interpretation of animal behaviour, as well as rudimentary geology and astronomy. With only two weeks to learn everything before a national exam, where a grade of 75% was required to pass, I was starting to think I'd bitten off a little more than I could chew.

So was my roommate. Bea had a lot riding on this. She'd made her living for many years sailing all over the world. Along with her ex-husband she would, by turns, captain the ship, and plan and prepare the meals, while hosting their upscale international guests. It was thrilling but utterly exhausting work.

"The thought of even buying the food and loading it on the boat for another trip is enough to make me sit down and cry," she confided. "I need to change my life. Understand, no?"

I understood completely. She was on her own, needing to find some stability on dry land. She'd invested every last cent in taking this course.

As exam day approached, the pressure was intense. I was feeling the strain, but for Bea, it was crippling. She stopped coming to meals. I'd wake up in the middle of the night to find her poring over her notes. When she saw that I was awake, she'd barrage me with questions:

"A spider is different from an arachnid, but they're both anthropods, no?"

"Yes, that's right, but I think you mean arthropods."

"No?"

"Yes, a spider is an arachnid, but not all arachnids are spiders. Yes, all arachnids are arthropods, not anthropods."

"I get so confused between Italian, Latin and English. I get my words mixed up. Now what about the trophic pyramid thing? That's all energy, no?"

"Yes, but Bea, I'm not studying now. I am trying to sleep, and you should too."

The day before the exam, she wouldn't come out of the room. I had to go and find a quiet place to study because her nervous energy and constant stream of questions made it impossible for me to concentrate.

I had really grown quite fond of her, so I checked in on her a couple of times and brought her a sandwich I knew she wouldn't eat. But there was nothing more I could do for her. If I didn't focus, I would fail too.

Then, at 6 o'clock, she emerged from our room. She was a woman completely transformed.

"I am not writing the exam," she announced calmly to everyone who'd gathered for dinner. "If I will write, I will fail. So I will not write. I will stay for the rest of the course, then I will get a job on a ship for a few months. I will study and I will take the exam when I am ready."

With that, she strode into the bathroom and took the first shower she'd had in days.

As expected, the exam was extremely challenging. I was the last to leave the exam room, using every minute of the allotted three hours to read and re-read the questions and refine my answers. I knew I couldn't afford to lose a single mark through carelessness.

When it was over, there was no time to dwell on whether I'd passed or failed. The next phase was about to begin: a week of track and sign interpretation.

We left our permanent camp and drove across the game reserve to the remote area that would be our new home – a cluster of small tents, a larger kitchen tent and an open-air shower and toilet. New duties were added to the work roster: filling drinking-water containers, hauling wood and lighting the fire to heat up the shower water.

I've never really enjoyed camping and have always been a huge fan of indoor plumbing, so for me this was a pretty big stretch, as was the course itself. I was supposed to identify tracks of animals I didn't even know existed. I'd never even heard of a civet, which looked like a cross between a cat and a racoon, or its cousin the genet, a more cat-like creature with a spotted body and stripey tail.

I had signed up for this course not realizing that even the beginners' level was far too advanced for me. It would take a miracle to get me through the week.

That miracle turned up in the form of Martin, an intelligent, insightful soul with a great sense of humour. He reminded me very much of my husband. He'd come to the academy to get an advanced tracking designation, and, luckily for me, we were assigned to the same vehicle.

We spent a week together, trying to decipher the clues left behind by the creatures roaming the bush. For Martin, an experienced guide and tracker, it came easily. He generously shared his knowledge and skills in reading tracks and signs, and during our evening campfire conversations, he taught me even more about reading the people around us.

Even with the support and encouragement of my new friend, I knew I was not up to the task of scoring the 75% required to pass level one. I took a page out of Bea's book and decided not to take the next exam. I struggled to come to that decision – it was the first time in my life that I hadn't followed through on something I'd started, but I had to acknowledge that I needed more time and more experience.

I could still get my field-guide certification without the tracking designation, so instead of spending a miserable day failing my practical, I had one of the best days of my life.

It was Shani's day off, and she was heading to the house she shared with Jock, the reserve ecologist. She invited me to spend the day with them – lunch, followed by the privilege of feeding the elephants.

Shani was one of the best teachers I'd ever had and one of the nicest people I could ever hope to meet. She had universal appeal. All the men in the class had a crush on her, and the women – both of us – wanted to be her friend.

For the last dozen or so years Jock had been working with a group of elephants that had been rescued after a brutal culling in the nearby Kruger National Park. This attempt to curb the elephant population was ultimately a failed experiment. Many older elephants were killed, leaving far too many young ones with no family and no guidance. These unrelated orphans were brought to Mabula in the hope that they would band together and create their own herd.

Under Jock's supervision, the plan was working. The daily feeding ritual not only provided extra nutrition, but it also gave Jock and the newly formed herd an opportunity to bond. The invitation to tag along on this mission was a unique opportunity to get extremely close to these beautiful giants.

"You know, I've only ever been really close to an elephant once," I told Shani. "There was a circus coming to town, and I was invited to a media dinner to promote the event. They'd set up the tables in a big barn, and just as we sat down, they led an elephant into the room. We were all so surprised! I couldn't believe the size of her. They walked her around the room so everyone would have a chance to get a close look at her.

"When they got to where I was sitting, the elephant

stopped. All I could think was that she must have sensed how thrilled I was to see her. Then she waved her trunk in my direction, smelling me, and then gently placed her trunk on my shoulder."

"What a beautiful story!" Shani exclaimed.

"Yes, right up until that point," I said. "Then she sneezed. That's why I can tell you with confidence that soda water gets elephant snot out of silk!"

Shani laughed. "I will definitely keep that in mind."

The next morning, we wished the others good luck with their tracking exam, and set off for Shani's place. As she pulled her compact two-seater pickup into the driveway of her and Jock's house, something caught her eye.

"Look up there," she said, pointing to a branch high up in a tree.

Much to my surprise, there sat a cat – not an ordinary house cat or even the bigger, stockier African wildcat. It was a larger lynx-like cat. I immediately recognized it from my mammal book – a caracal.

"You're lucky: Princess is back!" Shani exclaimed. "She hasn't been here for the last few days. I was afraid you wouldn't get to meet her. Come on in, she'll come down in a little while."

Princess observed us casually from her perch, clearly not as excited to see me as I was to see her.

"That's good – she's ignoring us," said Shani. "We don't want her to assume that all humans are friendly and approach them. She and her brother were raised by people, but they got too big to handle, so they brought them here. Jock's trying to get them to hunt, and reintroduce them to the wild. They're at opposite ends of the reserve now, and we're hoping they'll meet up with other caracals to mate. The brother was showing a little too much interest in his sister, if you know what I mean. We want to make sure the gene pool stays strong."

We went inside, and while Shani made coffee, I admired the colourful artwork that decorated the walls of the small kitchen. Then I read the signature on the pieces.

"Wow – you painted these? They're great!" I said.

"Well, they're okay. You should see Jock's work. I'll show you."

She went off and returned with a magnificent sketched portrait of an elderly African woman.

"This is absolutely beautiful!" I said. "He's so talented!"

"Yes, but try telling him that," she said. "Come on, let's take our coffee outside and see where Princess is."

Sure enough, Princess had made her way down from the tree and was lounging on the terrace wall. I wanted desperately to touch her but knew that wasn't in keeping with the plan to get her to ignore people.

"Can I get a photo with her?" I asked.

"Sure, get closer to her and I'll take it."

That snapshot became one of my favourite photos. I'm lying a few feet from this gorgeous cat, completely enthralled and grinning, while she is looking out at the horizon, ignoring me completely.

The sound of tires on gravel alerted us to Jock's arrival. He'd made the drive into town to pick up what we needed for lunch.

Jock was an intelligent, artistic, sensitive soul with a generous heart – but for some reason, he didn't want anyone to know that. I'd met him earlier in the week when he made an appearance at the camp during our track and sign course. He looked like he'd stepped out of central casting for the movies – tall, lean and tanned, with shoulder-length blond hair, a face etched with character and skin made leathery by too much time in the sun.

The reserve wanted to use him for their marketing. The problem was that they wanted him to be a friendly Steve Irwin Crocodile Hunter type, while he preferred to present himself as a bad-tempered crocodile.

When he turned up at our camp, the guys on the course were all eager to talk to him. He held court all evening, beer in hand, squatting by the campfire. (Jock rarely, if ever, used a chair, always preferring the floor or the ground.) I was far more interested in listening than speaking that night, so while he made a big impression on me, he concluded that I wasn't particularly interesting. Shani's endorsement was the only reason I'd been given a second chance.

Jock strode into the kitchen, depositing the grocery bags on the counter. We went in to greet him.

"So, I understand from Shani that you are, in fact, quite a worthwhile person," he said, with a wry smile.

"Thanks for the compliment, I think," I replied.

We unpacked the grocery bags and opened the wine. Shani and I made the salad while Jock cooked the prawns and made the sauces, one with butter and garlic, the other lemon.

Suddenly there was a commotion down the hall and Princess raced by, batting a roll of toilet paper between her paws, just as any house cat would do. It occurred to me that this was the most interesting household I had ever visited.

We sat on the living-room floor, enjoying the feast, discussing everything from art and music to politics and philosophy.

"You're a real Renaissance man," I said to Jock. "Gourmet cook, philosopher, lover of music, artist, elephant whisperer..."

"Well, elephant yeller, sometimes. Just depends on what they're up to. Speaking of which, we've had our feeding time, now it's theirs."

We piled into Jock's truck and headed to the storeroom to pick up the bags of nutrient-rich pellets that supplemented the herd's diet. We loaded three heavy bags onto the back of the pickup, then set off to find the elephants. Information from guides who'd been driving around the reserve came in over the radio, helping us to pinpoint their location.

When we arrived in the area where they'd last been seen, Jock put the vehicle in neutral, then loudly revved the engine several times – a sound the elephants knew meant dinner.

Jock jumped out of the driver's seat and Shani slid over to take his place.

"Shani will drive, I'll feed, and you can sit in the back with me, watch and take pictures," he said.

We climbed on to the flatbed of the truck, and Jock grabbed the first bag of pellets, slicing it open with a knife. He started pouring the contents on to the ground as Shani drove ahead slowly, creating a trail of food for the elephants to follow.

Suddenly, five grey giants materialized as if from thin air. I thought we would hear them coming, but not even the sound of rustling leaves or a breaking branch gave any warning at all. I marvelled at how creatures so big could move without making a sound.

They walked in single file, behind the truck, picking up the pellets with their trunks and scooping them into their mouths.

Jock opened the second bag and poured out the contents as the truck continued to lead the procession. When the third bag was opened, he dumped it all in one spot, and Shani parked the vehicle a few metres away. The elephants approached, still in single file, then broke rank and gathered around the big pile of food. I watched in awe, taking in their sheer magnificence.

The elephant's trunk is a wondrous thing. It's estimated to be made up of somewhere between fifty and a hundred thousand muscles. This versatile appendage can be used with great force to break off a large tree branch or with great dexterity to gently pick up small berries from the ground.

The large female in the group was waving her trunk in our direction, as she investigated our scent. She took a few steps toward the truck, and I was startled when she rested her trunk on the tailgate. A few pellets of food lay there, and she grasped them with the tip of her trunk and put them in her mouth. I had to remind myself that this was not a trained circus animal, but a wild elephant. I resisted the urge to reach out and touch her.

She turned and ambled back to join the others. Now that the food was finished, the younger bulls engaged in a bit of play-fighting while the matriarch and the other adults showed affection by rubbing cheek to head and intertwining trunks in what looked like a slow-motion dance. It was one of those rare occasions in life when time seemed to stand still, and nothing else mattered except what was happening in that moment.

I don't know how long we sat there before the spell was broken. The matriarch decided it was time to leave, and the grey ghosts melted into the bush once again.

Immediately after our elephant encounter, I was dropped off back at camp for one last night. Most of the students had done well in the tracking exams and had achieved at least a level-one designation. Bea, in particular, had excelled, attaining level two.

But the larger question remained: how many of us had managed to pass the national qualification exam we'd written the week before? Without that, the tracking designation meant nothing. We'd find out our results in the morning.

I woke up feeling anxious and excited – anxious about the exam results, and excited that Johann would be coming to get me in just a few hours. It had been an intense three weeks, and our communication had been minimal. I could hardly wait to see him.

I packed my bag and waited to be called into Shani's tent for the moment of truth. I wasn't feeling particularly optimistic. Several students had already been summoned, and had emerged from the tent looking angry or dejected. So far, only one had passed.

Shani poked her head out of the tent and called my name.

Her poker face didn't last long when I walked into the tent. She immediately broke into a huge grin.

"You did it! You passed!" she exclaimed, as she handed me my certificate and gave me a big hug.

In the end, of the sixteen of us who started the course, I was one of only four who passed.

I left the Limpopo Field Guide Academy with a certificate, but more importantly, with some new friends and an even deeper love and appreciation for the African wilderness.

I actually got job offers from a couple of lodges, but my immigration status wouldn't allow me to accept any of them.

Life had other plans for me, anyway.

11

Penetanguishene and Red Deer, Canada

April 2011 to February 2012

My mom had been diagnosed with breast cancer. She'd withheld that information from me for some time, because she knew I would want to go straight home, and she wanted me to carry on with my plan and take the Field Guide course. By the time she told me, she was about to undergo a lumpectomy to remove the tumour.

Following the surgery, she'd have to weigh her options regarding radiation and chemotherapy. I wanted to be with her to help her navigate the cancer maze but there was one problem: Johann still couldn't come with me.

Despite my supplications to the embassy in Pretoria, his paperwork remained bound in red tape. They were waiting on a security clearance from Sudan to prove that Johann's work there had been legitimate. The fact that he'd been there under a United Nations contract didn't seem to matter. In the pre-referendum chaos of South Sudan, we knew that a piece of paper for a couple of foreigners wasn't going to be a high priority for any government official.

We prepared ourselves for a long wait, and once again found ourselves saying a heart-wrenching goodbye at Johannesburg airport. I really hate crying in public and tried to keep my sobbing silent, but I wasn't too successful. The heaving shoulders were a dead giveaway, anyway.

Each time circumstances forced us apart, the goodbyes seemed to get worse. But despite the obstacles and the difficulties, we had no regrets. To this day, we still make a point of telling each other, "I choose you again today." I vowed that that would be the last time I would leave my husband at an airport, not knowing when I would see him again.

It was another boring flight, but at least the just-over-a-day-long journey gave me a chance to collect myself and focus on the positive: being with my family and friends again.

The plane taxied down the snow-covered runway at Toronto Pearson airport. It was good of Mother Nature to supply some snow for my return home. I got off the plane and joined the long line at customs. The agent looked at my passport, determined everything was in order, stamped it and said, "Welcome home." I almost made a comment that if the government would let my husband join me, it *could* be home again – but I thought better of it.

As I came through the gate, scanning the crowd, my mother's striking silver-white hair caught my eye. Next to her stood my father. They both looked a little worse for wear, with the stress of Mom's diagnosis and surgery, as well as the uncertainty of the choices that lay ahead. But when they saw me, their faces lit up. It was good to be home.

The ensuing weeks were a crash course in the big C. I spent many hours on the internet at the local library reading facts, theories, and what I'm sure were outright fabrications about effective treatment of breast cancer. We understood so little about the disease that we didn't even know what questions to ask.

We prepared as best we could, knowing that we had to go into the medical appointments having done as much research as possible in order to be able to make monumental decisions on the spot. The oncologists were overwhelmed with the number of patients for whom they were responsible, and they didn't have a lot of time to explain things. Sometimes details fell through the cracks.

That became clear at our first appointment with the oncologist. Mom had had her lumpectomy in January, but by the time we got to see the oncologist it was the end of March. The doctor was very surprised by the delay. According to protocol, Mom should already have had chemo and be starting radiation.

This news surprised my mom too. "But I thought that the radiation came first," she said. "Then I would decide if I want to have the chemo."

"No," said the doctor, "the chemo comes first, and then we do the radiation. There is a test we can do that will tell us if you're at a high risk of the cancer redeveloping. The test is expensive, about $5,000, but the government plan will pay for it. We can do the test, but you have to decide this right now: if the results come back that you are at a high risk, will you go ahead with the chemo? Unless you're sure that you'll undergo the treatment, it's a complete waste of money for us to run the test."

"I don't know. I need to think about it."

"I understand," replied the doctor, "but unfortunately, because it's taken so long for you to get this appointment, we're out of time. I need your decision this afternoon. Why don't you go downstairs to the cafeteria and have some lunch, then come back up and let me know what you decide?"

Over quiche on paper plates with plastic utensils, we struggled to come up with the "right" answer.

In the end, Mom felt that less treatment was better. The tumour was small and had been successfully removed. The margins were clear. She was 74 years old, and if the cancer should redevelop in five or ten years' time, she would deal with it then. She did concede to having the radiation, which for a woman who won't even take an aspirin was already a stretch.

We went back upstairs and declined the test and the chemo.

The doctor wasn't surprised.

"I understand your decision. Yours wasn't a large or aggressive tumour. If it does redevelop later, it's just as likely that you'd die *with* cancer, not *of* it."

The following week, the radiation treatments were underway, and we were all feeling comfortable with the decision.

With that crisis behind us, I turned my attention to waging an all-out campaign to get my husband into Canada. I wrote letters and made phonecalls to people who wrote letters and made phonecalls on my behalf. We just had to get the Canadian officials to waive the requirement for a security clearance from Sudan. We were being kept apart by one little piece of paper, and there didn't seem to be anything we could do about it.

Two more months passed, and I couldn't wait any longer to be reunited with Johann. I started looking for cheap airfares to Johannesburg. Before logging off my computer, I checked my email one more time. And there it was, the long-awaited message – Johann had been approved as a permanent resident of Canada!

He gave notice at his job, and we booked his one-way ticket.

We would finally start our new life together in Canada on the fourth of July. It would've been perfect had he been able to arrive on the first of July, Canada Day, but this was appropriate too – when we got together again, there would definitely be fireworks to rival the Independence Day displays in the States!

This time, it was my turn to meet Johann at the airport. We'd been married for almost a year, and I finally got to introduce my husband to my family and friends and show him my beautiful country.

My sister Giselle and her family put on a welcome feast fit for royalty. We celebrated our first anniversary over a steak and shrimp barbecue with my dear friends Lena and Norm. Lena had been my friend since kindergarten, and she and her husband had been together since they were teenagers. When my love life had me in despair, I looked to them as a shining example of how relationships could be. They were now approaching their 25th anniversary and still going strong.

My lovely friend Lynn, who's like family to me, threw a "Welcome Johann/first anniversary" garden party so that all my London friends could finally meet my husband. This event was extra-special, as it was there that Grandma and Caroline had their long-awaited and much-anticipated meeting with Johann.

"It's about time," said Grandma, as she reached up to give him a hug. "I'm 86 – how long did you think you could keep me waiting?" she teased.

Caroline was uncharacteristically quiet, but the look in her eyes said it all. She, too, had worried that Johann would make her wait too long and that the cancer would take its toll before she would get to meet him. She hugged him warmly and spent most of the evening sitting by his side. The party was a huge success, carrying on until the wee hours of the morning.

About a week later, we spent a gorgeous sunny day sailing on Lake Ontario with my friend Sarah, who also accompanied us on outings to the theatre and to see the amazing Cirque du Soleil. Her home was always open to us, and we enjoyed many meals and glasses of wine together. It was a social whirlwind, exhilarating and exhausting for both of us, and more than a little overwhelming for my husband. The exposure to so many new people and such an affluent lifestyle made it seem to him that the bar was set quite high for building a life in Canada.

Johann also went through his own version of culture shock. While I'd experienced trouble getting used to the barbed-wire fences and locked gates, he couldn't get over our lax security. He found the Canadian tendency to be law abiding a bit too good to be true.

One day we were driving to the beach and we passed a cornfield. The farmer had set out a table with some plastic bags and a cash box. The sign said "Corn – $2.50 a dozen". Johann started to laugh. "No way! That guy just leaves all this at the side of the road and expects people to take the right amount of corn and leave the right amount of money?"

"Yeah, that's how all the farmers do it here. And he'll have left some small bills and coins in the box so people can make their own change."

Johann just shook his head. "If you did that in South Africa, the cash box, the corn and the bags would all be gone. Hell, they'd even take the table!"

He was also thrown by our national tendency to be so friendly and polite. One day we were running a few errands at the mall. The grocery store was our last stop, and while I went to pay for the items, he went out to get the car. When he drove around to the storefront, he expected I'd be waiting at the curb, but he looked in the window and saw me still chatting with the clerk. When I finally came out and got into the car, he asked how I knew her.

"Who? The lady in the store? I don't know her."

"Really? You were talking to her like she was an old friend. All this random friendliness is going to take some getting used to. It makes me a bit suspicious."

We were starting to get the feeling that it wouldn't be easy for us to transition into a life in Canada. Johann's paramedic qualifications weren't recognized, but the health-and-safety courses he'd taken were internationally accredited. We kept hearing that this was a huge growth industry, so we felt sure it wouldn't be long before he found a job.

We moved in with my parents in my hometown of Penetanguishene, a couple of hours' drive north of Toronto. I went to work part-time for my jeweller friend, and Johann's fulltime job was looking for a job. After five months of sending out resumes across the country without securing a single interview, he was becoming very discouraged. I was afraid that if something didn't come through soon, he'd lapse back into a depression.

Then, one day, he opened his email and there was an offer. But it wasn't in Canada.

One of the guys he had worked with in Sudan was now running a medical clinic for an Italian oil and gas company in Mozambique. He proposed that Johann run the clinic every other month and get some experience doing safety inspections. The job wouldn't pay that well, but Johann reasoned that the experience, along with the words "oil and gas" that he could add to his resume, would make him more marketable in Canada, particularly out west in the oil patch. Canada is the fifth-largest oil-producing country in the world, and at the time, the industry was booming. There were high-paying jobs to be had in the oil fields in the north of the province of Alberta, if you could handle the isolation and the frigid temperatures.

Because of the one-month-on/one-month-off nature of Johann's new job and the visa requirements, we couldn't settle in Mozambique, so I couldn't go with him. We'd have to create a base in South Africa, and I'd be alone every other month. Unless I could find a loophole in the immigration law that would allow me to get a job before the required five years of marriage, I'd be destined to be on my own with no transportation, little communication, and even less money.

I could see how excited Johann was, but the knot I was feeling in my stomach was not excitement. It was anxiety. Johann had to leave for Mozambique right away. I couldn't believe this was happening again: we were going to be on opposite sides of the globe. I had vowed not to do that airport scene again, and I knew my heart couldn't take it.

On 15 December, I said my goodbyes to my husband at home and went off to work at the jewellery store, leaving my dad to do the airport run.

On 25 December, I flew out to Red Deer, Alberta to visit my good friend Kate. People say we look like sisters, and it sure feels like we are. She'd just undergone her seventh surgery in an attempt to repair an ankle shattered in a car-and-moose collision several years before. She could use my help when her teacher husband had to go back to work after the holiday break, and I was craving her company.

After a week of holiday feasts and fun, we settled into a routine: she'd spend the morning stubbornly trying to do household chores, while I spent the early part of the day working on an online Teach English as a Foreign Language (TEFL) course. I had no idea what the future held, but I hoped I'd be able to put the certificate to use wherever Johann and I finally settled.

By late afternoon – or sometimes even early afternoon – it was happy hour, and Kate and I would make ourselves cozy on her bed as we watched "guilty pleasure" television while sipping on beer, tequila or wine. We could almost forget that we were in Red Deer in January, and that it was forty below outside.

It was cold like I had never experienced before and hope to never experience again. It hurt my lungs to breathe, so I'd wrap a scarf around my nose and mouth to warm the air. The house's furnace just couldn't keep up, and icicles appeared inside the windows.

When Johann and I were chatting on Skype one day, I showed him the chunks of ice forming on the windowsill.

"That's inside?" he asked incredulously.

"Yup," I replied. "And just think, the experience you're getting now in Mozambique could get you a job in the oil-and-gas industry in Canada – and we could live in Fort McMurray, where it's even colder!"

He quickly changed the subject.

I had no idea what I would do when I returned to South Africa, and wondering what my friend from the Limpopo Field Guide Academy, Martin, was doing these days, I sent him an email. I knew he'd moved from Cape Town, and I thought we might make a home base where he lived now, wherever that may be. If I was going to have to be alone for a month at a time, I wanted to know at least one person.

I got a response the next day. He and his family were living in a little town called Hoedspruit. "You'll love it here!" he enthused. "We're right at the foot of the Drakensberg mountains, and the gateway to the Kruger National Park. It's a nice friendly little town. You'll fit right in."

Shortly after Martin's reply, I got an email from Shani. She'd just been offered a new job and would be moving to the same area.

Everything seemed to be falling into place. Through a friend of Johann's sister, we found a cottage to rent. We took it sight unseen, but I must admit we were a bit apprehensive after our experience in Kroonstad – if we could afford it, what must it look like?

Divine intervention can be the only explanation. We couldn't have chosen a better place than where we ended up at Ver End.

12

Hoedspruit, Limpopo, South Africa

February 2012

What's in a name?

I'd been told that in the black African culture, the naming of children is a privilege that is often given to the grandparents. And it's believed that a child who cries incessantly has, in fact, been given the wrong name. The only thing to do in that case is to visit the traditional healer, the sangoma, who will ask the spirits to reveal the child's rightful name. Then the child will stop crying.

Some babies are named with hope: Fortunate, Happiness, Sweetness, Smiling, Goodness, Gift. Others are named with aspiration: Justice, Remember, Civilized, Deliver. Then there are those who are named with humour: Surprise, Goodenough, Finished (the last in a long line of offspring) and, my personal favourite, Lazybones, who apparently didn't kick for the entire nine months of his creation.

I wanted to know more about these cultures, but it was proving difficult to get people to open up to me. I initiated conversations with the check-out ladies at the grocery store, the waiters at the restaurants and the vendors selling the mangoes, avocados and lychees at the side of the road. They were all unfailingly polite but not particularly receptive to going beyond the usual greetings and comments about the weather.

I suspected it might be much different in the larger cities, but here in this little town, while people got along and treated each other with respect, it seemed that blacks and whites just didn't mix.

There really weren't many black residents in Hoedspruit. Those who worked in the town crowded onto the big buses that came in from neighboring Acornhoek each day. Those who couldn't afford the bus fare would hitchhike. The reality was that most couldn't afford to live in the town, but even those who could afford to, chose to stay in the outlying communities where they'd grown up.

The person I felt I was most likely to forge a friendship with was Patrick, the young man who worked as the groundskeeper and general handyman at Ver End Lodge. He called me "Madam", and I noticed that he would never address me first, so I made sure I was dressed and ready to greet him early each morning as he performed his duties sweeping the walkway and tending the garden in front of our cottage.

When I heard the sound of his buffalo-thorn-branch broom sweeping the concrete walk, I emerged from the kitchen.

"Good morning, Patrick!"

His reply was a melodic "Hallooo."

"How are you?"

"I am fiiiine todayyy." He virtually sang his response.

Each day I tried to ask him questions about his life, but he seemed hesitant to share much. What I was able to ascertain over a period of about a month was that his native language was Sotho, that it took him over an hour to get to work by bus from his village, and that he wasn't married but had one son.

"Why aren't you married, Patrick?"

"I am too young."

"How old are you?"

"I will be 34 on Friday."

I playfully scolded him, "That's not too young! And your birthday is Friday? That's the same day as my husband's. It's also the day he'll be coming home. We'll have lots to celebrate!"

Patrick smiled and carried on with his work.

When I mentioned to Franz and Thelma that Patrick's birthday was coming up on the Friday, they were surprised and asked how I knew; it never occurred to them that he and I would be having personal conversations. I was surprised that he'd worked there for years but they didn't know his age or his birthday.

When Friday came around, I gave Patrick some chocolate, while Franz and Thelma honoured the day generously by giving him a huge sack of maize-meal. This is a staple food of the black African diet, and the gift was very much appreciated.

It became clear to me that while Franz and Thelma cared very much for Patrick, and he liked and respected them, there was an invisible line ingrained in all three of them, so they had never really thought of each other as friends. The dance between the races had changed since the African National Congress (ANC) government had taken over in 1994, but nearly twenty years later it seemed that no-one had figured out the new steps or who should lead.

It was confusing for South Africans of all races to know how to negotiate the new reality, and as a foreigner I struggled to know how to "be" in this place. My nature was to be friendly, open and helpful, but I'd been warned that to do so could be dangerous. "Don't pick up hitchhikers" is pretty sound universal advice, but when the hitchhiker was a young mother with a baby tied to her back, standing in the sweltering midday sun miles from town, shouldn't I have offered her a lift? If I saw someone lying next to the road, what kind of a person would I be if I just drove by?

That actually happened one day, but the experience did nothing to help me know how to answer that question. The incident caused an extremely tense discussion between Johann and me. We were driving in to town, and a young man lay apparently unconscious by the side of the road. My instinct was to stop, but Johann said no.

I was shocked. It took me well over an hour to try to process this, and to get my emotions in check sufficiently to be able to have a conversation with him about it. We had finished our errands in town and were on the road home when I broached the subject. I tried to choose my words carefully.

"I'm really troubled by what happened on our way in to town. I can't believe we just drove by that man. What if he needed medical attention? And shouldn't you as a first responder, of all people, feel a duty to stop? Also, he was lying almost in the road. What if the next car that came along was speeding and the driver didn't see him and ran him over? It would be our fault!"

Calmly, my husband responded, "First, I did look to see if there was any evidence of injury, but there was no blood and no apparent trauma. It's Sunday morning and the end of the month, which means he would have just been paid. His condition was most likely a result of too much fun last night. Believe me, working all these years in the ambulance, I've seen this plenty.

"And if we did stop, what could I do for him? I have no

equipment, no gloves and no protection for doing CPR. In a country where Aids is so prevalent, you can't take those chances.

"And if he were to be hit by a car, why would it be our fault? Why wouldn't it be the fault of the driver who hit him, or this man who put himself in that predicament in the first place? Why do you take so much responsibility for other people? Why do you think it's up to you to think for everyone else?"

"Well," I countered, "we could at least have moved him further off the road."

"Yes, love, we could have. But in doing so, we would've made ourselves very vulnerable. I'm sorry to say that sometimes this type of situation is a set-up. Someone lies down in the road and waits for a Good Samaritan to stop. When a person stops to help, the 'injured' man's buddies come out of the bush, and beat and rob the person who was trying to do the right thing. Sometimes they even do this with a doll wrapped in a blanket to trick you into thinking a baby has been abandoned.

"Yes, I agree, love, it's a sad state of affairs when you don't feel you can help your fellow man. But I am not willing to risk your safety or mine."

As we approached the curve in the road where the man had been lying, I was relieved to see he was gone. I never imagined myself to be the type of person who would leave someone lying by the side of the road, but that's exactly what I had done.

Even when the incident was long over, I still grappled with a way of coming to terms with this moral dilemma that presented itself in various forms on an almost daily basis. I had certainly learned one thing: it's never black and white when it comes to black and white!

My neighbours at Ver End were a lovely Afrikaans couple in their late 50s. Originally from Pretoria, they were fairly new to Hoedspruit.

A few years earlier, Oom and Tannie – Afrikaans for "uncle" and "aunt", and used as terms of respect for elders, even if they're unrelated – had decided to take a leap of faith and move to Wales so they could be near their daughter, who had emigrated there. It didn't take long before they realized that they had several things working against them. The rand didn't even come close to measuring up to the pound, and their life savings were disappearing at an alarming rate. Their age and limited English made it difficult to find work.

They'd managed for a few years, but in the end they'd decided it was best to come back to South Africa. They'd chosen Hoedspruit to be close to Oom's father. His health was failing, and they wanted to be able to help with his care. Oom picked up intermittent construction work where he could while they tried to figure out a new plan for what were supposed to be their golden years.

There is an Afrikaans pastime called *rondry* – literally, "driving around". Every weekend, the pair would jump into their car to see the sights. I had become quite friendly with them in the few weeks since Johann had left for Mozambique, so they invited me to tag along with them as they headed out one sunny Saturday afternoon. They had no particular destination in mind, so when I expressed interest in seeing the village where our gardener Patrick lived, we drove out to the nearest black township.

I was encouraged to see that the government was trying to make good on its promise of decent affordable housing. We came to a neighbourhood of one-room cinderblock houses. Certainly not luxury, but with solid construction and electricity wired in, these structures were much better than the cobbled-together tin shacks where so many lived out their days.

We continued down the road, passing small houses with front gardens. The children who were outside playing would stop and stare. They obviously weren't used to seeing white faces in their neighbourhood, but when I smiled and waved, they would grin and happily wave back.

At the end of the road, we got to the construction site of a school project where Oom had been working for the last few weeks. The new school was a modest structure consisting of just two rooms with a flat roof and no plumbing. There was no infrastructure for water in the area, so eventually, when enough money had been raised for the project, they would have to dig a well. They'd erected a large tin canopy to serve as an outdoor classroom, providing better protection from the rain and the blistering sun than the large tree that had been serving that purpose.

I was surprised to find out that this school was being financed by a Canadian. I took a few pictures and decided to find out more about the project, who was financing it, and if there was anything I could do to help.

Heading back down the road, we stopped at a roadside stand in front of a squatters' camp where an elderly black woman sat in the shade of a big marula tree, appropriately selling beer made from the marula fruit. The beer had been bottled in one-litre plastic Coke bottles. The caps hadn't been put on because the beer was still fermenting.

At only R10 a bottle, it seemed like quite a bargain, so we decided to buy some, despite the objections of Tannie, who thought we were crazy, and that we'd end up having a marula-beer explosion in the car. After a bit of negotiation, it was decided that we'd buy a bottle but we'd put it in a plastic bag in the trunk of the car in case the lid blew off.

"In Australia, they have wine from Bin 555," I joked. "In South Africa, we have beer from Tree No 3."

With our cargo safely stowed, we pulled back onto the road, right behind a maddeningly slow driver. Oom became very irritated, and after a few minutes completely lost his patience.

"Is it a black driving?" he asked. When a coffee-coloured hand eventually poked out of the window, he felt vindicated. "I hate them." He all but spat the words.

His wife was embarrassed. "You mustn't say that," she scolded him, looking sheepishly at me over her shoulder.

"Ah yes," he replied, remembering the Canadian in the back seat. "She still thinks they are human beings."

There was an awkward silence as our eyes met in the rearview mirror. Oh, how I dreaded these moments. I wished they would stop coming up, but realistically I knew we were probably a generation or two away from that.

My first instinct was to challenge the statement and tell the racist why he or she was wrong. But I hadn't grown up here. I hadn't experienced either side of this equation. I hadn't known oppression, nor had I been the victim of violence. I truly wanted to understand, not to judge. I knew judgment on my part would be sheer arrogance, so I decided to say nothing for the time being.

We left the township behind and carried on to Swadini, a holiday resort where locals can buy a season pass to enjoy the tennis courts, miniature golf and swimming pools. There is a cold pool and a warm pool – although, of course, these terms are relative, depending on which part of the world you're from.

"Will you go in the cold pool?" Tannie asked me.

172

"For me, it's probably not that cold." I stuck my foot in to test the water and immediately jumped in.

Tannie came slowly down the ladder, balking at the temperature.

"This is what you get in the middle of summer in Canada – it's really quite warm."

She shivered and looked at me like I'd lost my mind.

After about ten minutes, she'd had enough of the cold, so we climbed out and plunged into the "warm" pool. It felt like hot bathwater, so I only lasted a few minutes.

We went into the change room to dry off and get dressed. I noticed the black patrons chose one side of the room, while the whites went about their business on the other side.

We returned home late in the afternoon, and sat out on the verandah watching the birds and monkeys. There was a commotion nearby, and suddenly a young impala burst through the bush, easily outrunning whatever had been stalking it.

The marula beer had now been in the fridge for about an hour and we decided it was cold enough for us to give it a try. The Coke bottle opened with a hiss, and Oom half-filled two glasses – we'd decided to start slowly as we didn't know how our stomachs would react to this concoction; it was hard to say what kind of quality control they might have at Tree No 3. The beer was quite bitter but had a refreshing taste that reminded me a bit of sour grapefruit juice.

The time seemed right to open the discussion I felt I needed to have.

"What you said earlier about the blacks – can we talk about that?" I asked, and added, "I freely admit I haven't walked in your shoes, so it's very hard for me to understand."

"Sure," he said. "You see this scar?" He traced the long crease running along the outer corner of his left eye and down his cheek. "This is what I got when I was at a convenience store picking up a loaf of bread. I was about to pay when a black decided that he was next in line. When I disagreed, this was his response."

Oom went on, "One day we were driving to work and we stopped at the traffic light. Out of nowhere, this man appeared and reached in the car window. He grabbed the gold necklace my wife was wearing and pulled hard. Luckily the clasp broke, but her neck was badly bruised and blood poured out of the deep gash it left.

"The resort we were at this afternoon? I took my daughter and her fiancé there for a weekend when they visited us from the UK. We checked into our chalet and decided to go for a quick swim. We were only gone about fifteen minutes, but we got back in time to see a black running out the back door with a big knife in his hands. If we'd been away a few minutes longer, we would've lost our computer, our cellphones and the little cash we had.

"I don't think you'll find a white South African who hasn't been robbed, beaten, stabbed or had a gun pointed at them. If you do find one who hasn't, that person will know someone who has. And if it happened to you? If you were beaten or raped? Would you be able to forgive?"

"I don't know," I said, "but that's a separate issue from race. I don't think that it would be any easier for me to forgive a white man who raped me."

He considered that a moment, then said, "That's fair. But a black man would probably give you Aids."

"As could a white man," I countered.

"Not as likely, but yes," he conceded. "You must understand, it's all about experience. We have had terrible things happen to us, and in each case, the person who did it was black."

"Sure, but look at the difference in population – ninety percent of South Africans are black, so the sheer numbers just make it much more likely that an assailant will be black. And I don't think people are being targeted specifically because they are white, but because they have money. Many black South Africans are still very, very poor. Would you rob to survive? I think I would."

"I can see that you think I'm terrible, but I am getting better, you know. Two years ago, I wouldn't have gotten into that swimming pool as I did today, because blacks were in it. I know this is the 'new' South Africa and it will never go back to the way it was, but where do you draw the line?"

"I don't know what you mean. Draw the line about what?"

"So you have blacks and whites swimming together. Now they're in schools together. Then your daughter comes home one day and tells you she wants to date a black. They fall in love, get married and have a baby. Now you have a coloured child. Whose fault is that?"

"Why is there a fault in this situation? Why is there blame?" I asked. "To me, there's only a child, born from two parents who love each other. Isn't that all that matters? Who cares about the origins of the parents? People just are who they are. In some ways I think that may be the only solution – we mix our bloodlines so much that there's no more black or white."

"You could be right," he said and refilled our glasses.

13

Hoedspruit, South Africa

February 2012

I wasn't sleeping well. I'd tried lots of techniques to quiet my mind, but none of them had worked. I missed my husband and worried about money. I mentally subtracted the time difference between Canada and Africa, and thought about my family and friends, especially Caroline.

There could be no more denying it. Caroline was dying. I felt overwhelmingly sad to realize that I would never see her again.

It had been almost three years since she was diagnosed with cancer. Doctors had first detected it in her breast but then discovered a multitude of tumours on her liver. With the liver cancer so advanced, they'd opted not to operate on the breast. The prognosis at the time was less than six months.

But Caroline had absolutely refused to accept that prediction. She'd endured countless rounds of radiation and chemo of various types, with one purpose in mind – to live as long as possible for her boys, then aged 7 and 9.

A little over two years ago, she'd bought a life-insurance policy that would only pay out if she managed to live a full two years after the purchase.

"Do you think I'll make it?" she'd asked one day as we took one of our short walks around her neighbourhood.

"I know it seems a long way off, but you will make it – and then some."

"Okay, I will."

She'd made it.

I felt deeply privileged to have been part of her journey. I will never forget the joy of her surprise 40th birthday party, or the intimacy of shaving her head when it became too painful for her to have hair on her tender scalp. We'd spent many hours sitting in her living room on the cream leather sofa, sipping tea and trying to make sense of this wonderful/difficult/joyful/painful thing called life.

I know she'd enjoyed being on my journey too. She'd said she was living vicariously through my adventures – the trip to Sudan, then the trials and tribulations of falling in love with a man who lived halfway around the world. She had so looked forward to the day when Johann would come to Canada and they could finally meet, and she'd been so happy for the chance to get to know him when he finally did arrive for those few months.

When it had all seemed too improbable or impossible, she was my biggest supporter. When I couldn't decide if I was brave or totally insane to take the chance and turn my whole world upside down, she'd steadfastly insisted it was brave. Turns out it was a little of both.

As our friendship grew, so did our faith. Spiritual exploration was something we both enjoyed. She was what I would term a modern traditionalist, while I was a little more "out there", embracing New Age teachings. She'd been my sounding board as I worked my way through *Conversations with God* (the first three books of which I read three times each), and the writings of Eckhart Tolle, Louise Hay, Iyanla Vanzant, Wayne Dyer and ancient texts like Lao-tsu's *Tao-Te-Ching*.

The basic message is all the same: we are love, without end, and the Eternal Moment of Now is all there is. Caroline, better than anyone I know, lived in gratitude in the present moment. If I ever manage to have half her grace, I'll have come a long way.

Saying goodbye when I was leaving Canada had been difficult, both of us knowing it would probably be our final visit. She said she hoped this was a very short-term arrangement and that Johann would find something in Canada so that we could return home soon.

This was the hardest part of living so far away – missing out on precious time with people I love. Grandma was 86, and had also expressed the fear that we wouldn't ever see each other again. My parents, both well into their 70s, were also anxious for me to return home.

The last communication I'd had from Caroline brought the very distressing news that her doctors were saying she was nearing the end of her life journey. I'd written to her several times, but she hadn't responded so I knew it was happening fast. I'd been trying for a while to set up a Skype date with her, but I sensed she really didn't want me to see her. She didn't know how beautiful she remained in the eyes of those who loved her.

I wondered how many weeks it would be until I got the message I was dreading.

With that last thought, I knew I wouldn't get to sleep, so I turned on the TV and watched *CSI* reruns until the wee hours of the morning.

I woke up a few short hours later as the birds' dawn chorus began. The raucous francolins started things off, with the Cape turtledoves the next to join in. They seemed to be singing their name: *Cape TUR-tle, Cape TUR-tle*.

"Chic-weeou, chic-weeou," chimed the black-backed puffbacks.

"Ka-waayyy," called the aptly named Grey Go-away-bird.

What to do at 5am? Yoga, of course. The temperature had been pushing 40 degrees Celsius all week, so if I didn't do it early, I didn't do it at all. I knew "hot yoga" was all the rage, but for a premenopausal woman who was starting to experience hot flashes, I figured that was just looking for trouble.

As I came up from my downward-dog position, I noticed something black on the stone wall. I went to take a closer look – was it mould? How could it grow so fast? I looked around the room and spotted more of the same on the ceiling. What on earth could it be?

"What the hell are you?" I asked out loud. When the stuff refused to answer, I went next door to ask Tannie, who would surely be more responsive.

I poked my head through her open kitchen door. "Could you come and have a look at something for me? I seem to have something black growing on the walls and ceiling in my bedroom."

"Ah, I think I know what it is – termites!" she said, and reached into the cupboard under the sink, pulling out a spray bottle filled with a milky liquid.

We walked along the green concrete pathway that led to my house. When we reached the bedroom, her suspicions were confirmed.

"Yes, termites. See, these are actually little tunnels they are making."

She sprayed the black columns and they immediately dissolved, running down the walls in dark muddy streaks. "Just let that dry. You can clean it up later."

At least it wasn't a dangerous invasion, and it seemed to be an easy fix. I sprayed all the little tunnels and washed away the residue. I went to bed that night thinking the problem had been solved, but I woke up the next morning to discover that it had, in fact, multiplied. There were more tunnels everywhere – on the walls, on the ceiling, and sticking straight up on the floor. Now they were all over the house. I found them in the hallway, the lounge and the kitchen.

I popped in on my neighbour again.

"Howzit?" she asked, using the most typical South African greeting.

"Not great. I think yesterday's crew were the scouts. Today we have the full invasion."

Tannie grabbed her trusty bottle and some rubber gloves, handed them to me and said, "Well, I guess you know what you're doing for the rest of the day."

I sprayed everywhere. Then the power went out. Ugh – loadshedding, one of the banes of South African existence. When there isn't enough electricity being generated to meet the demand, the provider pulls the plug in certain areas. Today apparently it was our turn. Or maybe it was something worse, like a substation failure. I hoped for loadshedding – that would only last for a few hours. A bigger problem could keep us in the dark and without refrigeration for a few days.

With no fans to dissipate the fumes from the spray, the smell was overwhelming, so I had to go outside. Hours later, the chemical smell still hung in the air. Even when the power came back on and the fans were running, the fumes still lingered.

I took a good book and went to the jackalberry tree in the front yard, first scanning the overhead canopy for snakes. I couldn't see anything, so I settled in, counting on the birds to sound the alarm should anything start to slither in the branches. There was a green vine growing up one of the trees in the garden, and at first glance it looked like a boomslang – literally translated, a tree snake, which sounded benign but happened to be one of the deadliest snakes in the region. I jumped every time I saw that vine, and I resolved to cut it down before I gave myself a heart attack.

I heard some rustling in the rafters of the car port. *Oh, what now?* I wondered, and was greatly relieved when I looked up to see my squirrel friend Scrat running along the beams with a branch in his mouth. He was in the process of building a nest on the ledge above the door of the neighbours' house.

He ran back to the tree for more building materials. He started gnawing at a stem, but it wouldn't break. He decided to use leverage. He took the leaves in his mouth, and pulled hard in an attempt to break the small branch. I cringed because I could see he had literally bitten off more than he could chew, and I wished I could tell him to let go. *Oh, little guy, this is not going to end well. You need to take it slow – one small twig at a time.*

That's an important lesson I was still trying to learn: don't try to tackle everything at once, but take it one step at a time.

Powerless to impart this wisdom to the tiny tree-squirrel, I waited for the inevitable. As predicted, instead of breaking, the branch shot back to its original position, catapulting Scrat right out of the tree. He lay on the ground, stunned – but only for a second or two, before giving his head a shake and climbing right back up to tackle the branch again. I guessed that that was the wisdom he had for me: when life knocks you down, shake it off and get right back at it.

It was starting to get dark outside before the fumes had dissipated enough to allow me to go back into the cottage. Armed with rubber gloves and a bucket, I took on the near-impossible mission of washing the black mud from the white walls with our brown floodwater. It took me a couple of hours but finally the place seemed habitable again.

I went next door to return all the supplies I'd borrowed from Tannie. My timing was perfect. Finally, something went right that day. She was just removing vetkoek from a pot of boiling oil on the stove. I couldn't resist those light fluffy doughnuts that she filled with cheese and savoury ground beef.

She kindly handed me a couple of the warm pastries to take home.

"I know you think you're done, but wait till you wake up tomorrow morning," she warned. "Then you'll see who else was hiding in your house."

I have no idea how many cockroach corpses I swept up the next day.

It seemed there was always some kind of battle to be waged in this place. Franz says we're all fighting what he calls "the civilian war". He explained his theory to me one ridiculously hot afternoon as we drove into town with the air conditioning blasting. Despite the unit's best efforts, we were still only getting moderately cool air from the vents. We'd decided to go into town to pick up a few groceries in the hope that the AC in the store would be working so we could get a least a half-hour's reprieve from the relentless heat.

"Every day we must fight to survive," Franz had said. "We fight with nature, we fight with each other. We fight to pay the bills and put food on the table. We fight for the most basic services – water and electricity. Most of all, we fight to be who we are. It is always a struggle. It's terrible. I don't know what is wrong with the world." He leaned in and paused for effect. "You know, people have died today who have never died before!"

This little quip caught me completely by surprise and I laughed out loud. "Oh, that is shocking, Franz. You know, dying doesn't scare me, but after listening to you, living sure does!"

"It's hard, Jax, it's hard."

"Do you think it's possible that because you keep saying it's hard, it becomes so?"

"No. It doesn't matter what you say. It's just hard."

As much as I tried not to view life here as a struggle, it did seem that way sometimes. We were often under siege. After that last incident, I'd added "termite patrol" to my daily routine of vigilance. It was getting to be a fulltime job, staying on top of everything: checking for venomous sac and violin spiders in the folds of the curtains and the bedskirt, checking between the sheets for the same spiders or the more remote possibility of a scorpion or a snake, ironing underwear to kill mango-fly larvae...

When I'd first heard about this, I thought it was a joke, but it was no laughing matter. I was informed that when you hang out your laundry to dry, sometimes these flies lay eggs in your clothes, particularly in underwear. If you don't kill them by either tumble-drying your washing (of course, we didn't have a dryer) or ironing it, they could burrow into your skin and you'd have to make a trip to the doctor to have the maggots removed. The area south of the bikini line definitely wasn't one where I wanted someone digging around with a needle! To my great relief, I learned the flies were only around for a short period once a year.

Yes, living in the bush came with its share of challenges. While the majority of South Africans feared their fellow man, we had nature to contend with – but I still thought it was a good trade-off for not having to live behind iron bars and barbed wire in an urban area. In either scenario, it seemed to me that the key was to learn, understand, let go of fear and find a way to coexist in harmony.

That was the South African dream, the vision held by Nelson Mandela and Archbishop Tutu: a Rainbow Nation where there was room for everyone. Nearly two decades after the end of apartheid, that vision remained but it was blurry at best. It seemed to me the caste system was still deeply entrenched, but the perceived hierarchy depended on which race or in some instances even which tribe a person belonged to.

While the segregation barriers had been officially removed, the separateness remained. There were white neighbourhoods and black townships, with the Coloured people living in areas of their own.

While for the most part the groups didn't live together, they did work together. Where Johann worked when we lived in Kroonstad, it seemed to be in a state of uneasy truce. He was employed by a private ambulance service where the paramedics were of different races. They all seemed to get along well, but Johann was the only white medic who would associate with his black colleagues outside of work. His black ambulance partner was a guest in our home, but we were never invited to his.

We did drive out to his place one day to pick up a case of beer he got for us. The prices of food and liquor in the townships were much cheaper than the prices in town. As we drove through the streets of his neighbourhood, we couldn't help but feel conspicuous, and when we got to the house, he met us at the driveway and we weren't invited in.

When it came to job opportunities, the racism pendulum had gone from one extreme to the other. Despite being qualified and well experienced, because he was white, Johann couldn't get a job with the provincial ambulance service, which pays much better than private services. Affirmative-action programmes had been designed to give opportunities to those who'd previously been denied them, but they also had the unfortunate effect of creating another class of disadvantaged when it came to seeking employment – in this case, the white South African male. My husband and those like him now found themselves at the bottom of the hiring hierarchy. This is why Johann had ended up working in remote locations – first in Sudan, then Mozambique, where his talents were valued and he received a living wage.

For us, being apart was a huge sacrifice, but we hoped the experience he was gaining would eventually lead to a job that would allow us to live together *and* pay the bills. That was our dream, but I was starting to wonder if it could ever come true in South Africa. It felt it could be a very long time before the racism pendulum came to rest where it should be: exactly in the middle.

While the races all had their struggles to contend with, as a foreigner, I had one of my own, and it was all in my mind. I remember learning in elementary-school science class that the brain is divided into two hemispheres, left and right. It now occurred to me that mine was further divided into hemispheres in the geographical sense: north and south; or, as I called them, my African brain and my North American brain.

My North American brain was a real whiner. It mourned its many perceived losses and dwelled in the place of "used to". I'd be going along just fine when it would suddenly rear its ugly head to say something like, "You used to have unlimited high-speed internet at home and you could communicate with anyone, anywhere, any time.

"You used to have a car you loved, and you could afford the gas to put in it to go anywhere you wanted.

"You used to have a great social life; you were never alone unless you chose to be."

My African brain knew that I was a very lucky girl. While I may not have had an internet connection at home, I had access to the internet in town, and friends who would either give me a ride or lend me a vehicle to get there once or twice a week.

Was I lonely? Hell, yes! But I had an amazing husband, a supportive family, and wonderful friends who all loved me. It just so happened that none of them was there at the moment.

I always found the complaints of my North American brain annoying, but sometimes they were downright embarrassing. "You used to have beautiful furniture that actually matched! And don't get me started on the bed... You used to have one of those fancy Tempurpedic mattresses, and now, when you do finally get to sleep, you wake up because of the spring digging into your hip."

When my African brain regained control, I was mortified to have even had those thoughts. I was warm, dry and fed. I had a couch to sit on and this one didn't even smell of cat pee! I slept on a bed, not on the floor.

Yes, there were people of all races in South Africa who lived the affluent North American lifestyle, but the vast majority struggled far below what would be considered the poverty line in that other world north of the equator and across the ocean. There were people just down the road from me living in tin shacks with no plumbing and no electricity. When I considered their situation, it seemed not only absurd but obscene to listen to my North American mind complain about shabby furniture – or anything at all.

14

Hoedspruit

February 29, 2012

It took a day that normally didn't exist for the improbable to happen. I finally had an appointment with the elusive internet guy!

My neighbours had warned me that having an appointment with him, and his actually turning up, were two completely different things. They'd been waiting for the semi-mythical satellite-TV guy for about eight months at that point.

I knew I shouldn't get my hopes up but then I had to believe that if a miracle were going to happen, it would most likely be today, February 29th, as though the universe had opened a golden window of opportunity. I decided to remain unabashedly optimistic. He just *had* to come.

I decided to set up a chair in the front garden under a tree and wait there with an eye on the road to be sure I didn't miss him.

Communication was both expensive and challenging in this part of the world. When we heard about a new internet service provider that had a better signal and cheaper airtime, we jumped on that opportunity and drove the hour to Tzaneen in a rental car to buy a modem and lots of airtime.

We got the modem home and tried to install it. Something wasn't working. We called the helpline and they walked us through the procedure. Still no luck. So we asked for the tech to come out.

We were given a case number and told to wait for a phonecall that never came. We called. We emailed. The answer always came back the same: we'll call you and set up an appointment. But the phone mocked us with its silence.

After Johann had been gone a week, I started to get desperate. It was bad enough being apart, but not being able to communicate with him, or with my family and friends in Canada, made it so much worse.

I called the company again, but this time I wasn't going to hang up before I got a real answer. I told the customer-service representative that I would be quite happy to wait on the line all day, until they could give me an appointment. Not knowing how to deal with me, she eventually put me through to her supervisor, who promised they would definitely call me back this time.

Another week passed, with more phonecalls and more emails on my part, and still no appointment.

I was now three weeks into this ordeal. I was out of both red wine and patience.

I called again, determined not to hang up until a firm appointment had been set. I spoke to the supervisor again, and through sheer stubbornness finally managed to make it one rung higher on the bureaucratic ladder: the supervisor's supervisor earnestly assured me that they would call and make an appointment. He sounded so sincere, I believed him. Then the miracle happened: a few hours later the phone rang, and with great pride, the date and time of the appointment were announced.

And that miraculous day was finally upon me! The fabled internet guy was scheduled to be arriving at noon. I was absolutely giddy at the thought that I could be Skyping and instant-messaging later that very afternoon – amazing! I vowed I would never take those privileges for granted again.

A little burgundy Volkswagen slowly turned into the driveway.

I leapt out of my chair. Could it be?

It was! The internet guy! And right on time too!

A slight young man climbed out of the car. I wanted to hug him.

Instead I extended my hand. "Hello! I'm so glad you're here! I'm Jacquie."

He smiled broadly and shook my hand. "I am Rodanzi," he said. "But please, don't be too glad to see me until we know if I can get this working."

I offered him something to drink, and asked if he wanted to use the facilities before he got down to business.

"Yes, please. I was going to use the side of the road, but then I saw this miniature crocodile thing. Then I thought about snakes and I decided to keep driving."

Rodanzi told me that he'd grown up in Pretoria and didn't know much about the bush. Finally, here was a chance for me to share my nature-guide knowledge.

"The crocodile-like thing is a monitor lizard. He prefers food he can swallow whole, so he wouldn't be too interested in you. As for the snakes – they make me nervous, too, but apparently no more nervous than we make them."

The look on his face told me that Rodanzi was not convinced. "That's all well and good," he allowed, "but why take chances?"

With that, he turned and headed into the house to use the washroom.

He soon returned and began to unpack his bag of tricks, an array of gadgets that surely would be able to solve any problem. Then he got to work. He tried everything he could think of to get the modem to connect to the network. He tested my SIM card in his modem and his in mine. He switched modems. His fingers flew across the keyboard as he attempted no fewer than a dozen different procedures, but with no success.

194

After about forty-five minutes he was forced to admit defeat. "This just isn't going to work," he said glumly. "I'm so sorry but the signal just isn't strong enough out here."

I was deeply disappointed, and I didn't want to accept that verdict. "But we asked if it would work here in Hoedspruit and they said yes. I thought your company had a deal with the other big company that has a tower on the mountain over there."

"We do, but only up to a point. When their system gets busy, they flip a switch and it cuts us off. You're now enjoying the benefits of that arrangement."

"Benefits?"

"Yes, being cut off," he replied, and we both started to laugh.

"I know it's a long drive and you have no vehicle, but I think you must find a way to go back to the store to try to get your money back. If you go through customer service on the phone, you'll be waiting for a very, very long time to get a refund."

"Well, it shouldn't be a problem getting my money back, right? We asked if it would work here and they said yes."

"You haven't lived in Africa very long, have you?"

He packed up his things, and we shook hands again. I thanked him for coming such a long way and for trying to be helpful.

As I watched him drive away, I noticed the model of the car. It was a Tenaciti – the perfect car for South Africa, where it seems it takes tenacity to get anything accomplished.

Despite my despair over the internet situation, I couldn't help but smile. It had been such a pleasure to meet that young man. He was educated, bright and funny. He dashed my hopes for better communication, but he gave me a glimmer of hope for the new South Africa.

The lousy internet signal at our house was a very good reason to drink, either out of frustration or as a solution.

I had discovered a wonderful pub in town called the Safari Club. They had cold beer on tap and free wifi there, so when I couldn't stand the "whichever way the wind blows" signal and I could find a lift, I'd head into town. I'd install myself on a couch near an electrical outlet, plug in and order a beer. I sipped very slowly, while emailing and surfing the web like mad. The owner, Gavin, didn't seem to mind.

On this particular day I'd hitched a ride into town with one of my neighbours. I'd seen an article in the local newspaper about an art exhibition at the gallery in town. Of course, by the time I saw the article, the opening night had come and gone, but I thought at least I could still go to look at the paintings.

I decided to go to the Safari Club first to send an email to my sister and catch up on the news of the world. I settled into my usual spot and ordered a Black Label draught, the most popular beer in South Africa – which, interestingly, was created in Canada in my adopted home city of London. South Africans never believed me when I told them this fascinating fact, but a Google search always backed up my claim.

As I sat there sipping and surfing, I caught what sounded like a Canadian accent. Two couples at the next table were discussing how difficult it was to pick out any familiar words when people were speaking Afrikaans, and what a tough language it was to learn.

I honestly hadn't intended to eavesdrop, but I couldn't help but interrupt.

"Excuse me, but... you sound like me! Where are you from?"

"Canada," came the reply.

"Where in Canada?" I asked incredulously.

"Red Deer, Alberta."

"You're kidding! I was just in Red Deer for Christmas before I came back to South Africa. I went from temperatures of minus 40 to plus 40 in one day!"

"What were you doing there? Do you have friends there? Where are you from? So you live here now?" The questions came pouring out in the delight of this surprise encounter with a fellow Canadian.

I gave them the short version of who I was and how I'd come to be in the Safari Club in Hoedspruit, Limpopo, South Africa on a Sunday afternoon. I told them about Johann being in Mozambique, and our ongoing quest to find the one thing that would change everything for us – a decent-paying, stable job for Johann in the health-and-safety industry.

"Well," said one of the men, "you had to come halfway around the world to meet a guy from Red Deer who can help. I'm going to give you the name of a friend of mine. He's the president of a big health-and-safety operation headquartered in Calgary, with an office in Red Deer. Have Johann write to him."

We continued to chat as the couples finished their lunch. The men expressed their regret that they'd arrived in town on a Sunday, so they couldn't buy beer. I took them to the local shebeen, a tavern where you can buy beer any time, even on public holidays. The bar smelled of stale spilled alcohol and the music was loud, but the beer was cold and cheap, which more than made up for the ambience.

Once they had their supply, we exchanged contact information and said our goodbyes. They were heading off to a lodge for a few days, then would go on to Joburg and Cape

Town before heading back to Canada. The man promised to contact his friend on our behalf when he got home.

I considered going back to the pub to email Johann about this surprising turn of events, but decided to wait. He'd be home in a few days, and I could tell him in person.

Much to my surprise, I was feeling ambivalent. Part of me was excited. A fulltime job with a decent salary is what we'd been hoping for. But at the same time, I didn't feel ready to leave Africa. Both times I'd lived here had been a bit like living in solitary confinement, but this time felt different. Yes, the obstacles of transportation and communication needed to be conquered but they weren't insurmountable. I really felt that we could build a life here. This small community, with a population of less than five thousand souls, seemed to be a magnet for interesting, creative people from all over the world. Writers, artists and photographers were drawn here because of the stunning natural beauty and, of course, the magnificent wildlife. You can't help but be inspired here!

I continued with my original plan and walked over to the art gallery to see the paintings and hopefully channel some of that inspiration. It was dark and locked up tight. Of course – it was Sunday in a small town. Disappointed, I went back to the pub to wait for my ride home.

I woke up the next morning, determined to see that art work. For some reason I felt positively compelled. I went around to all the neighbours to see if anyone was heading into town, and luckily I found a lift.

Armed with the newspaper article about the artist, I walked into the gallery and stopped in my tracks. The most stunning mural of colourful African figures grabbed me by the heart.

I stood staring, and I'm pretty sure my mouth was hanging open. Soon, I was aware of someone standing next to me. I glanced over, and did a double take. I looked at the photo in the newspaper article. Yes, it was her.

"You're the artist!" I exclaimed.

"Yes, that's me," she confirmed with a melodic Scottish lilt.

We spoke about the mural for a few minutes then she asked, "Is that a Canadian accent I detect?"

"Yes, well done! Most people guess American."

"Well, I have an advantage. My dad spent a long time in Canada. He loved it. When I was growing up, he used to sing me the Canadian national anthem every night before bed. I still have relatives there," she explained. After a short pause, she said, "Would you like a tour? I can tell you about the work."

I was totally captivated by the images Anne had brought to life; the colour and movement perfectly expressed the essence of life in Africa.

While art had always been a part of her life in Scotland, moving to the tropics had really fired up her creativity. She, her husband and three children had lived in Papua New Guinea, South Africa and Australia before deciding to relocate permanently to South Africa. Since settling here, her technique had evolved, and now the intense colours of the land, the sky and the clothing of the people jumped off her canvases. It was such a pleasure to hear her story and feel her passion.

"You obviously love art," she observed, "and this is an incredible place to fuel your creativity. You must start coming to my class."

"Oh, thanks, but no. I do love art but I don't think I can create it. I can take a good photograph but when it comes to drawing I don't know if I have any talent at all."

"You won't know until you try, and you might surprise yourself. If you take good photographs, you have a good eye. And there's so much more to art than drawing. Lots of great painters can't draw. And besides, you can make some new friends. My Tuesday-morning class is a group of lovely and interesting women. Oh, and one of them lives quite near you, so I'm sure you can catch a lift."

I left Anne and headed back to the Safari Club, where I'd arranged to meet Martin for a drink while I was in town. There was a spring in my step as I strode over to my usual spot, where I found him waiting for me. I excitedly told him all about meeting Anne, and how thrilled I was by her art and the prospect of joining her class.

"That's great, Jax," he said, "and quite a coincidence. I just heard that your new friend is heading up an English and adult literacy programme at Tanda Tula, one of the safari camps where I freelance as a guide. It's a great opportunity for you to teach, and it'll get you out into the bush. Tell Anne that you've got your qualifications. I'm sure she'd be happy to have your help."

The following Tuesday morning, I made my way to art class, feeling both elated and intimidated. Anne greeted me warmly with a hug and introduced me to all the women seated around her big dining-room table. They were all welcoming and friendly.

Once she'd given the lesson and the assignment for the day, and everyone had settled in to work, she came over and sat beside me.

"I hear you have your qualifications to teach English as a second language," she said.

"I do! How did you know? Small-town grapevine, I guess?"

"Yes, except here we call it the bush telegraph." She laughed. "I'm going out to Tanda Tula again next week. Come with me. I've been doing some preliminary testing to figure out how many levels we have to teach and who belongs in which group."

"Oh, Anne, I would love that! But I don't know how I can do this without a car."

"Yes, I know that's an issue, but I think I can help you. Come see."

She led me out into the driveway and indicated an old beat-up white Opel Corsa convertible. "It's a bit rough around the edges, but it'll get you there. If you can pay for the insurance, you're welcome to use it."

For a split second I thought of the sexy red BMW convertible that had been my pride and joy in my previous life. How I'd adored driving that beautiful car! But through my new South African eyes, this car looked just as good.

"It's perfect!" I exclaimed. "Thank you so much!"

I woke up early the next morning and jumped out of bed. This was it! At long last, day thirty had arrived! While it had seemed interminable, our month apart was finally, mercifully coming to an end. Johann was on his way home and would be arriving that night.

In that moment I could truly appreciate my good fortune. After all, most people only get one honeymoon, but the advantage of our situation was that we got one every other month.

I resolved not to think about the flip side of that coin for another thirty days, when it would be time to say goodbye once again. I missed Johann so much when he went away, but in those moments of terrible loneliness I always reminded myself to be grateful that I had him to miss.

It would be late, at least 10pm, by the time he arrived, so I decided to find ways to fill the day getting ready. I started by sweeping the house and mopping the floor. The water was black with dirt. Ah, the joys of living in the bush. It took three mopping sessions to get the water to improve to its usual colour, post-flood light brown. No, actually it had improved to a light rusty orange. *Now that's progress!* I thought.

I figured this was a good time to do laundry. It would be lovely to have clean fresh sheets on the bed, and this was a chore I'd been avoiding for quite a while. Washing sheets and especially towels by hand in the bathtub wasn't my idea of a good time. Again, I always had to remind myself that I was lucky: I had indoor plumbing and a big bath; it's not like I had to lug the stuff all the way down to the river and beat it on rocks.

The wringing-out was the hardest part of the process, but once that was done and I'd got everything hung out to dry on the line, I felt a big sense of accomplishment. I stood back watching the orange-tinged formerly white sheets flapping in the breeze.

Then the only thing left to attend to was me. I had to admit I'd let myself go for the last month. When you spend most of your time by yourself, living like a hermit at the foot of the mountain, there doesn't seem to be much point in doing anything beyond brushing your teeth. I ran myself a dirt-tinged bath and settled in to shave my legs, thinking this could take a while. Then I washed and styled my hair. I even put on some makeup for the occasion.

Finally, when I looked in the mirror, I recognized that woman. It was only then that I realized that I hadn't looked or felt like myself since Johann had left.

And so the day passed. At last I was clean, smooth and feeling quite sexy. I was oh-so-ready for my man's arrival.

He sent a text message saying he was nearly home. I quickly slipped into the lingerie that he loves to see me in, and smiled at the memory of shopping for it. When Johann was working in Sudan, he'd had some pretty miserable birthdays. As his birthday approached during the year we were carrying on our torrid email courtship, he told me about the previous year, when on his birthday he and another guy were out in one of the armoured vehicles. The vehicle broke down and they sat there for the entire day in the sweltering sun with no food and very little water. It had been a memorable birthday, for sure, but not in a good way.

I'd wanted to do something to make his upcoming birthday special, but I was stuck for ideas. What could I possibly do for him when he was once again out in the middle of nowhere? Then I thought of something: I could send him some photos.

I called a photographer friend who often does sexy glamour shots and asked if she could help. After a fun excursion shopping for lingerie, I found myself in her studio wearing a little black teddy trimmed in cream lace. But as I stood there so scantily clad, I suddenly wasn't sure this had been such a good idea after all. Feeling awkward and embarrassed, I tried to back out, but with my friend's encouragement and a few glasses of red wine, Johann's birthday gift was soon ready to send. He'd got quite a surprise when he opened his email that morning!

He'd be pulling into the carport at any minute, so I quickly lit candles and pulled the two wine glasses we owned out of the cupboard. I'd splurged on a bottle of wine for this very special occasion; tonight, box wine just wouldn't do.

Then it dawned on me: Johann had been travelling since early morning, driving hours from the camp to the airport, flying in to Johannesburg, then doing the five-hour drive to get home. Would he be in the mood? Maybe it wasn't fair of me to ambush him like this.

I saw the headlights of the little car pulling up in front of the house. To hell with fair! I raced to the door to greet him.

His eyes lit up and he smiled that beautiful smile. He dropped his bag, swept me into his arms, and headed straight for the bedroom. Apparently he wasn't too tired!

The sun shone through the cracks in the blinds and the birds were chirping happily when I awoke. It was 8am. By some miracle, I had slept a full eight hours! Clearly, my battle with insomnia was over, at least for the next month, anyway.

Johann hugged me and we lay there, revelling in being together again at last. It was so good to have him home.

He got up and made a pot of coffee, and we moved out onto the porch and sat watching the birds. There were tiny blue waxbills and the much bigger bulbuls with their crested heads and little yellow bottoms flitting in and out of the birdbath.

I told Johann about the Canadians I'd met and the chance of a job for him in Canada, then about Anne, the art and the opportunity for me to be a volunteer teacher at Tanda Tula. He could tell how conflicted I felt.

"Never mind, love, no need to stress about any of it now," he said. "There's no decision to make at the moment, so just go ahead and do what makes you happy. I'm sure it won't be long until it becomes clear which path we should take."

I knew he was right, and wondered for the millionth time why I kept feeling the need to plan and make decisions, when experience had shown me time and again that life always managed to take care of itself. My job, as always, was to let go of my need to control, and enjoy the journey unfolding before me.

I couldn't have imagined the life I was now living, much less planned for it, but there I was, surrounded by the wilderness I'd grown to love in this most amazing place, with the partner I'd dreamt of for so long. So why not trust whatever force it was that had brought me this far to take care of what would happen next?

I understood that concept. Maybe, with time and practice, I would get better at living it.

15

Timbavati Game Reserve, Limpopo, South Africa

April 2012

It was a Monday morning, and I had given myself plenty of time cover the seventy-five kilometres between home and Tanda Tula luxury safari camp in Timbavati Private Game Reserve. From the first trip I'd made to teach at the resort, I'd learned that I had to factor in extra time – not just because the speed limit through the reserve was a tortoise-like fifty kilometres per hour, but because I wanted to drive in at a leisurely pace and enjoy the scenery, as well as the animals and the people I was sure to meet along the way.

I looked forward to the beaming smiles of the guards at the checkpoints. They'd grown accustomed to seeing me each week and had dispensed with the formalities of making me sign in and write down my registration number. When I got to the first control gate near the airport, Evans and the other guards would grin, wave and even bow graciously as they indicated that I may pass through.

These gents had a very tough job. They had to be alert and vigilant, checking for behaviour that raised suspicion and searching vehicles they suspected might be coming into the park to shoot with more than just cameras.

They really suffered on hot sunny days. The small guardhouse had no plumbing, so they couldn't even get a glass of water. I always made sure to bring extra water both on my way in and on my way out of the reserve. They kept a plastic cup by the gate so I could fill it up as I went by.

When I got to the second gate, which was the main gate into Timbavati, I'd exchange pleasantries with Orance, Johnson or Clifton. They always greeted me warmly and were delighted by my poor attempts at conversing with them in their native xiTsonga.

Once I'd passed through, I'd be on the lookout for the usual suspects. Generally, the vervet monkeys would hang out in that area. They could be real pests, but if they weren't trying to steal your food, the blackfaced bandits were pretty adorable. Sometimes, if I was lucky, I'd come across some elephants.

That day, I was in luck.

As I crested a hill on the dirt road, I saw another car at a standstill. I soon recognized it as belonging to our friends and neighbours, who were doing research at Save the Elephants, a nonprofit organization originally founded in Kenya by British zoologist Dr Iain Douglas-Hamilton in the 1990s to help fight the illegal ivory trade. Appropriately, they had stopped because of an elephant.

Make that a group of elephants. An entire herd that had been enjoying tender green leaves for breakfast was now making its way, one by one, across the road. They weren't in a hurry, so we couldn't be either.

I switched off the engine, wound down the window, and sat being lulled by the sound of rustling leaves and breaking branches as the elephants selected their preferred morsels. I listened to the low rumbling sounds they made as they spoke to each other in a language I wished I could understand. Of course, even if I could've understood it, I would only be privy to half the conversation; many of the sounds elephants make are at such a low frequency that they can't be heard by humans. In fact, it's suspected that other elephants detect these rumbling sounds as vibrations through their feet, making it possible for elephants to carry on a conversation even as far as twelve kilometres apart.

As I watched the majestic giants move slowly across the road, I couldn't help but compare this to the traffic jams I'd experienced as a city dweller. There, being idle for fifteen minutes would cause your blood pressure to spike. Here, it puts you in a relaxed, almost meditative state.

Eventually, the last of the herd crossed the road, and our two cars continued on to our respective destinations, knowing that no-one would be the least bit annoyed at our being a few minutes late.

Tanda Tula in the language of the local Shangaan tribe means "to love the quiet". This luxurious tented safari camp, the oldest in the Timbavati, is a sanctuary for Africa's Big Five, and for those who travel there to visit them. The scenery is stunning, the food exquisite. But it's the people who live and work at Tanda Tula that make this a truly special place. Many of them were now my students, and this divine spot had become my second home. I referred to it as my Disneyland, my happiest place on earth. It had been my privilege to become part of this family.

The adult-literacy programme was flourishing. It had started because the owners of the camp, Nina and Don, had wanted to create a Tanda Tula book club. It quickly became apparent that many of the staff wouldn't be able to participate because they couldn't read or write in their own language, much less in English. Some of the younger workers were better educated, but the older women, in particular, had never been given a chance to learn.

They were being given that chance now, and didn't hesitate to jump at it. Three times a week they faithfully gathered around the dining table on a big verandah where we created a makeshift classroom. Mongoose and antelope often observed the sessions from the front lawn.

The first time I'd stood at the whiteboard to give a lesson, I'd felt sheer happiness. I was sure that this must have been what my great-uncle Ernest had felt when he taught in

Nigeria. I knew that I was exactly where I was supposed to be, doing exactly what I was meant to do – at least for now.

This type of teaching was not an exact science, and it would've been so much easier if I understood the local language of the Shangaan tribe, a dialect of xiTsonga. I was doing my best to learn from my students but I'd managed to master only the most basic greetings and a few key words like "drink" and "water". But the small efforts I made to communicate in their language were rewarded tenfold by their delight in my less-than-stellar attempts.

It was a good exercise for a couple of reasons. It reminded me how hard it was for my pupils to learn English, and I suspected it made them feel much less self-conscious about making mistakes when they tried to speak English. After all, they couldn't do worse than my bastardized versions of their words.

So, how to teach literacy with a language barrier? Just start with the alphabet and see where it goes, I decided.

I wrote the first three letters on the board, and said their names: "A, B, C." I was met with blank stares. For several days, I tried to teach the alphabet, but I just couldn't seem to break through.

Try as I may, I couldn't understand why they didn't understand. I went to seek out one of the rangers in camp to see if he could shed some light on the situation.

Foremen had quickly become one of my favourite people of all time. He was gentle, kind, quick to laugh and always ready to help. He was also extremely bright, and his command of the English language would put many native speakers to shame.

When he came to class, it was to work on his written English. Because he'd learned to speak by listening rather than by reading, he found it difficult to know which spelling to use when the words sounded exactly the same but the spelling was completely different. He was already making great strides in that area.

I hoped he'd be able to help me with my stumbling block. I found him sitting on the porch outside his room, and he greeted me with his warm smile and a big hug.

"Howzit, my friend?" he asked.

"Overall, things are great, but I have a problem I think you might be able to help me with."

I explained the alphabet situation. "I really don't understand it," I said. "They can all write their names, but for some reason, I can't seem to make any headway teaching them the alphabet. I really don't know what I'm doing wrong."

"Ah," he said, "I think I see the problem. They don't understand what those letters actually are."

"What the letters are? I'm not sure I know what you mean. If they can write their names, they must have a basic understanding of the alphabet."

"Actually, no, they don't realize that those are letters. Let me see if I can explain it." He thought for a moment, then continued, "In their minds, they're not writing their names. They've been shown what their name looks like, and for them, it's a picture that they have learned to copy. They're *drawing* their names."

What a revelation! Suddenly, the whole picture changed.

Now, the question was: how would I teach the concept of an alphabet? The solution proved to be surprisingly simple, and was readily available in the lounge at the lodge. I searched through the board games that were there for the guests to use in the down time between game drives. Finally, I found what I was looking for: the box marked "Scrabble".

Armed with my new understanding and the letter tiles from the game, I approached my next class with confidence. I laid out the 26 letters of the alphabet in a row on the long table, and had the women gather around.

"Okay," I said. "We are going to write your names."

Elita was first.

"Your name starts with this," I said and slid the E out of its slot, placing it below the row of letters. "It sounds like its name: eee.

"Next is the L. it sounds like this: lll. When you put them together, it says eee-lll. That's the beginning of your name: El-ita."

And so we carried on through all of their names: Elita, Jenneth, Lindiwe, Girly, Thembisile and Melina. They all giggled with delight as they finally understood that these letters were not pictures, but symbols with definite sounds that could be put in different combinations to create words.

It was a transformational moment for all of us. Now, they could learn to master the tool that would allow them to learn how to read.

I loved my role at the camp, and felt I was growing into it more with each session. The drives in and out of the game reserve were as interesting and rewarding as the time with my students. Each trip was a new adventure, and I just couldn't get enough.

I knew a little about the animals because of my nature-guide course, but there was so much more to learn. Each time I saw a giraffe, for instance, it was a different experience. Sometimes they were alone, other times in groups. There was always something new to observe, sometimes subtle behaviours but in other cases glaringly obvious.

He was tall, dark and handsome. Most of them are. But the females in the tower of giraffes I sat watching seemed to sense that the approaching stranger was a particularly desirable mating partner. If I hadn't known better, I'd have sworn they all stood a little taller and batted their ridiculously long eyelashes in his direction.

The two males in the group also knew this guy was hot stuff and that he meant business, so they instinctively cleared off as Handsome made his way toward them. That left a line-up of ladies eager for a closer inspection by the newcomer.

He sniffed the hindquarters of the first female to determine if she was in heat and ready for mating. Nope, she wasn't the one, so he approached bachelorette number two in the same manner: he sniffed her, then contorted his face into a grimace to pump the hormones she exuded into his Jacobson's organ, a scent organ situated on the roof of his mouth which he used to detect the hormones that would tell him if she was ready for love. This time, he got the answer he wanted – she was in heat.

After a few moments of nuzzling, it was apparent that these two wanted some time alone, so the rest of the giraffes moved on, leaving the new couple to get better acquainted.

I'd witnessed this scene on my way in to camp, so as soon as I got there, I went to find Foremen to ask a few questions about courtship in the world of giraffes.

"Will they mate right away?" I asked. "I was tempted to follow them. That would have been something to see!"

"No," he replied. "He may have chosen her, but she still has to choose him. He'll be waiting for a few days at least. He'll follow her around like a lovesick puppy until she decides that he's persistent and fit enough to mate with. Remember, having a little one is a big undertaking for her. She'll carry for fifteen months, so she has to choose a mate wisely."

"People can learn a lot from giraffes," I observed.

Each time I made the ninety-minute trek from our little cottage by the mountain through the Timbavati Game Reserve out to Tanda Tula, I fell a little more in love with the animals and the people. I couldn't imagine how things could get any better.

Then they did.

The lodge was becoming more and more successful, and in addition to the regular guests, a couple of special groups were coming in, and they needed some extra help. The owners asked if I wanted to help out in guest relations by hosting the special groups, which would mean living out at the lodge for a few months while Johann was away.

It was a dream come true for me. Beyond my hosting duties, when there was time and space on the game drives, I could go along to take photos and write for the company's blog. It was perfect: I could use my journalism skills and get more experience as a nature guide.

This time, when it was time to say goodbye to my husband, it was a completely different scenario. He drove me to the lodge and got me settled in to my staff-quarters room. He'd be off to Mozambique again the next morning. It was still hard to see him go, but now I had something to look forward to, and I knew this time our month apart would fly by.

I had a hard time getting to sleep that night, because I was so excited about getting ready for my first guests the next morning. It was a group of Australians coming in to celebrate a special birthday, and I wanted everything to be perfect. I'd never been employed in the hospitality industry, but I hoped that hard work and enthusiasm would compensate for my lack of experience.

I was headquartered at Tandala, a small lodge at the other end of the property from the main lodge. It was normally the residence used by the people who owned the land the camp was built on, but it was also sometimes pressed into service to host private groups. The Australians would join the main-lodge guests on game drives and at breakfast, but would have lunch and dinner at Tandala, culminating in the big 60th-birthday celebration.

I was awake early and got down to Tandala just as my helper arrived. Tracy was the wife of Jeffrey, one of the trackers – the guy who sits on the front of the Land Rover looking for the tracks and signs that will help the guides find animals on game drives. She was young, bright and lively, and

I knew immediately that we'd work well together. This was going to be fun!

We spent the morning getting the place cleaned and organized, and while we worked, Tracy tried to teach me a few more phrases in xiTsonga. "You'll be speaking like one of us before you know it," she said, being overly generous with her praise.

The morning flew by and soon it was the time the guests were due to check in. We were ready.

"I'm sure they're going to be impressed," Tracy said. "And I think this is a good group for you to start with. I mean, they're 60, so they probably won't keep you up really late."

"You've never spent any time with Australians, have you?" I asked. "They're pretty much the most fun-loving people on earth. From my experience, a 60-year-old Australian can be hard for most 30-year-olds to keep up with."

The minute the group walked in, I could tell my theory was right and I knew I wouldn't be getting much sleep until they were gone. They were full of high spirits and energy.

The three days flew by, and because they were having so much fun, it was impossible not to join in.

Before I knew it, we were preparing for the main event: the birthday party. Tracy and I set the table outside, and hung white lights in the trees. We ventured into the bush to find branches, flowers and seedpods to use as table decorations. As the daylight faded, we lit the candles and the lanterns. The bonfire crackled. It was perfect.

Soon the unmistakable sound of the Land Rover engines alerted us that our guests were returning, and it was time to pop the corks from their frosty bottles and pour the champagne. As the vehicles pulled up to this romantic scene, our guests gushed in delight.

The meal was served and declared delicious. The wine and the laughter flowed freely.

Just when it seemed things were starting to wind down, the very creative birthday tributes started. A special song, a poem and a somewhat disturbing but hilarious finger-puppet show were presented to honour the birthday girl.

When the last rounds had been drunk, and the guests were heading to bed, the guest of honour came up and took my arm. "Thank you so much for everything you and everyone here have done to make this an unforgettable celebration," she said. "It's been positively magnificent."

"Oh, I'm so glad you feel that way! I'm completely new at this, and you're my very first guests."

She looked quite surprised. "I would've thought you've been doing it for years. I think you've found your calling."

"Well, maybe one of them. I also love teaching, writing, and being out with the animals. I never dreamed that at nearly 49 years old, I'd have so much trouble deciding what I want to be when I grow up, or be so excited about so many possibilities!"

"Good for you," she said. "And do what I do when someone offers me a choice between this, that or the other. I say, 'I'll have them all.' Who says we have to choose?"

16

Timbavati Game Reserve

May 2012

I woke up the next morning feeling content. It was already sunny and hot, and I had a leisurely morning ahead of me. The Australian group would be leaving, and after I'd seen them off, I wouldn't be responsible for another group for a couple of days. With any luck, I'd get to go out on a couple of game drives.

My room was a bit of a mess. It had really just been a place to change my clothes and sleep these last few days, so I gathered up all my laundry and threw it in a basket to take down the path to the laundry room.

I've always had a fear of snakes. I'd read the books, taken the nature-guide course and spent some time with our local snake and reptile expert in the hope that if I understood them better, I wouldn't be so afraid. And I wanted to be mentally prepared because I knew it was just a matter of time before I'd find myself face-to-fang with a venomous snake. Mercifully, it wasn't something that happened often, but when you live in this area, it's all but inevitable.

At that moment, I was still blissfully unaware that today was my day.

The laundry basket was quite full, and I was struggling with trying to keep the towels from falling out as I rounded the corner of the reed fence that separated the laundry room from the office. When my focus returned to the path, I saw it, straight ahead and just a few feet in front of me: a huge Mozambique spitting cobra.

I gasped and stopped dead in my tracks. The snake rose up, rearing its head and displaying its impressive hood. This is what's known as a startle display. I wasn't sure who was more startled, the snake or me.

Now what? I struggled to keep my wits about me. *Okay – think. What am I supposed to do now?*

We were both motionless for what felt like an eternity. Then I remembered: *I'm supposed to back away slowly.*

I was afraid to move and at first my brain didn't seem to be communicating with my legs but I tentatively took one step back, then another, never for a second taking my eyes off that puffed-up hood and darting tongue.

The bush seemed eerily quiet and I held my breath as I waited to see what would happen next. If it decided to spit its venom, I would most certainly be hit. I knew it aimed for the eyes, and at this close range it was sure to find its target.

Abruptly, the snake dropped back down to the ground, then reversed and quickly slithered off in the opposite direction.

"Just like it said in the book!" I exclaimed out loud. "Thank God I came across a snake who'd read the same book!"

I dropped off the laundry, and headed back toward my room. This time, a welcome sight came across my path. My neighbour in the staff quarters was a ranger nicknamed Scotch for his love of Johnny Walker, particularly Blue Label. But that was just one of his many nicknames; he was also known as the Elephant Man because his last name, Ndlovu, means elephant.

Of all his claims to fame, however, he was probably best known as the Bird Man. Scotch had a passion for birds and could name any of the six hundred or so in the area at just a glance or the sound of a call. That was impressive, but what really astonished the guests was his photographic memory. Scotch had committed the entire *Birds of Southern Africa* book to memory.

At the beginning of every drive, he would hand the book to one of the guests, and then as we went along, he would point out all the birds.

"Lilac-breasted roller," he'd declare when he spied a flash of turquoise and mauve in a tree. "Page 263, number one."

The guest with the book would dutifully flip through the book to the appropriate page and confirm that he was right. I'd never seen Scotch get one wrong, and the guests were always suitably impressed. His reputation had spread across the country, even reaching the people who'd published the book. When they released a revised edition, they sent a new copy to Scotch, along with a letter of apology for having had to change some of the names and page numbers.

"Hey, umfazi!" he yelled cheerfully, using the Zulu word for woman, as I approached. "You want to come on drive? I have room for you today."

"Not a question you ever have to ask, indoda," I responded in kind. "The answer will always be yes!"

I still had a couple of hours before our 3.30pm departure, so I went into my room and found my book of mammals. I settled on my bed to read up on lions. I'd heard they were in the area, and the guests had been treated to a good sighting on the morning drive. I hoped we'd be able to track them down again this afternoon.

I was engrossed in my reading when I was startled by a sound at the bathroom window. Someone was trying to come in! I caught a glimpse of a hand pushing on the window. It must be Scotch, I thought, playing a joke on me.

Then the hand reappeared, and this time I got a better look. That was not a human hand – that was definitely a big baboon!

It's one thing to have mischievous vervet monkeys in camp, but baboons are something completely different. When it comes to creating chaos, they're in a class of their own. You have to chase them out right away or they'll come to think of the camp as part of their territory and an excellent place to stop in for a meal.

I knew this guy would not be alone and it was important to chase him and his companions away, but that presented two problems: baboons aren't afraid of women, and this woman was very afraid of baboons.

I closed the bathroom door and looked out the front door. I could see the troop running down toward the guests' tents, so I ran as fast as I could along the staff-quarters path to find help. I found it in the form of one of the bartenders, a strapping young man named Smiling, and alerted him to the situation.

He quickly grabbed the slingshot and some rocks that were stashed under the bar for this express purpose, and set off to scare away the baboons. The sight of this man charging at them with the slingshot in his hand quickly changed their minds about ransacking the tents. Baboons seem to have a very good memory, and just seeing the slingshot was enough to make them turn and run. They left the camp without a single shot fired.

As if the cobra and the baboons hadn't provided enough excitement for one day, I was now about to experience my first real brush with the brutal world of lions.

We set off to the location where the big cats had last been seen that morning. Because it had been such a stiflingly hot day, Scotch assumed they would have hunkered down in a shady spot and spent the day sleeping. He was right. We spotted the four tawny figures lying in the tall grass.

These lions were well known to Scotch and all the rangers in the area. They belonged to the so-called Machaton pride – the group that had ruled and roamed our section of the Timbavati for many years. Their status was now being challenged by two big males who'd banded together and come in from the neighbouring Kruger National Park looking for a territory to take over.

The takeover process involved chasing away the adult males and killing any cubs. While this seemed incredibly cruel, Scotch explained there was a biological imperative for it. The new lions were compelled to remove the bloodline of the previous dominant males, and start populating the area with their own offspring. Killing the cubs served two purposes: the first was to eradicate the old bloodline, and the second was to bring the conquered females into heat. Once they've lost their babies, nature makes sure they quickly become ready to mate again.

At this point in the takeover, the Machaton males had been chased away, and the remaining pride members had split up and fled in opposite directions. The group we were watching now consisted of the grandmother, the mother and two cubs. They'd already been roaming the area for weeks but were no closer to reuniting with the other group, a female and two cubs that had recently been spotted at the other end of the territory.

To the human eye, the situation seemed heartbreaking.

"Don't you wish you could just sedate these four, put them in the Land Rover and take them to reunite with the rest of the family?" I asked Scotch.

He thought for a moment before replying. "Sure, you wish you could change the course of these things, that's how humans are. We always want to interfere, and think that we know what's best. But you just have to step back and let nature take its course. Nature is the mother of us all and she has much more wisdom than we do."

"I know that they're only doing what lions do, but I can't help but think of these two new males as the bad guys, and I don't think I will ever like them."

"Wait until their first cubs are born. That will change your mind. You'll come to like them, I promise you. It's like everything in life. There's a big change, a lot of emotion, and eventually you have to adjust. In time, it all feels normal again."

My own life experience had told me that he had that right.

It was always a treat to go out with Scotch. He was fun and easygoing, and I always learned so much when we went out together. He enjoyed having me along too. His formal education had ended in grade three, but he knew the bush like the back of his hand, and when it came to entertaining the guests he was second to none.

While he'd mastered much more than the basics in English, he sometimes struggled when trying to explain more sophisticated concepts. If he was trying to explain something to the guests and they didn't quite understand, I could explain it in a slightly different way. That would also give him new language to use the next time around.

"See, umfazi," he'd said, "that's what makes us the A Team! The elephant man and the leopard lady."

I was getting a reputation for being a leopard good-luck charm because more often than not, we'd have a great leopard sighting when I was along on the drive. I was quite enjoying my new nickname and its benefits!

While I adored the leopards, I remained intrigued by the lions. Just as Scotch had predicted, in time I did start to get used to the two big boys who'd successfully executed their takeover and were now firmly in charge of the territory.

My time living out at Tanda Tula had come to an end, but I scheduled my teaching days back to back, and was often allowed to spend the night so I could continue to write blogs and take photos. One day after class, Scotch reported that one of the big males had been seen mating with one of the Machaton females.

Lion mating is no quick affair; in fact, it's a marathon. The process goes on for three or four days, and the act occurs almost like clockwork at fifteen-minute intervals.

When we set out that afternoon, Scotch drove back to the area where the mating pair had been seen that morning, and that's where we found them. Male and female lay utterly exhausted a few metres from each other. Scotch cut the engine and we sat waiting for the next round, knowing it wouldn't be long until the urge struck again. Soon the male stood, yawned and stretched. He walked toward the female, but she wasn't ready quite yet. She gave him a swat across the nose with her enormous paw. He didn't seem to take offence and lay down next to her.

When she decided it was time, she raised her rear slightly. He didn't miss his cue. He stood, yawned and stretched again. He then walked behind her and mounted her unceremoniously. She appeared to be completely indifferent to the whole process, knowing that it would be over in thirty seconds or less. After about twenty seconds he was finished. He gave her a quick bite on the ear, possibly a payback for her earlier swipe at his nose. Then he resumed his position in the grass next to her.

"Well, wasn't that romantic!" I quipped.

"Not by our standards, no," said Scotch. "But that's typical lion behaviour. It's pretty serious business. They don't eat or drink for days at a time, just mate. With any luck, it won't be long before we have some new cubs."

Lion sightings were always special, but I was still eagerly anticipating the most special sighting of all. I was hoping to see the fabled white lions. These extraordinary cats with creamy-white fur and laser-blue eyes were rare, but the Timbavati was where I'd be most likely to find them.

In the Shangaan language, the name Timbavati translates to something like "to come down (like a bird) to the ground". According to legend, this is the place where a mysterious white star landed after plummeting from the heavens. The monarch of the area, Queen Numbi, approached it, saying that the star was a god that had come for her. As she neared it, she was engulfed in white and blue light, then disappeared. The star then rose into the sky. It was observed later that animals in the area were producing white offspring with blue eyes, most notably a pride of lions.

There are other versions of the story claiming that the lions either fell from the stars, or were the children of the sun god. While their origins are disputed, it seemed everyone agreed that these extraordinary animals were a rare and

232

beautiful gift to behold. If I was lucky, one day I'd have my chance to see them.

When the opportunity finally came, I almost missed it. I wasn't scheduled to go out on the drive that afternoon, as I'd recently started tutoring the lodge owner's young son, and had a lesson scheduled with him. Scotch found me chatting with some of the guests in the lounge and he came running over, literally vibrating with excitement. He'd just heard over the radio that the white lions were back in the area.

"You have to come, my friend!" he insisted. "It's been almost a year since the last time we saw them!"

My heart soared, and then immediately sank.

"Oh, Scotch, I want to go so badly, but I just don't think I can. I'm supposed to be tutoring in half an hour."

"You can't miss this," he reasoned. "Don and Nina will understand. Go ask them. I'm sure they'll let you go!"

"I don't think I'd better."

"Do it!" he cried.

I walked up the hill to their home and found Nina on the porch.

"Neens, I have a really huge favour to ask. I know I'm scheduled to tutor this afternoon, but the white lions are back in the area...."

"Go!" she cried. "Hurry, go now! Of course you can't miss this!"

I raced back down to where all the guests were climbing on to the Land Rovers.

"Wait for me, Scotch – I'm coming!" I called.

He gave me a big smile and a thumbs-up.

I raced back to my room and grabbed my camera. We had to hurry, or it would be getting dark by the time we got to the sighting. It was a long way off, but we were determined to get there before we lost the light.

Dusk was nearly on us when we caught our first glimpse of the five figures sprawled out just a few metres away from the carcass of a large buffalo. Even in the fading light, their white fur was striking.

The lions had been feasting all day, and were having a rest between courses of that massive meal. There were three tawny-coloured males, and two white females lying intertwined, bellies full to bursting, with mouths open and eyes closed. I already felt like I'd found the Holy Grail, but when one of the females opened her piercing blue eyes, I thought I must be in the presence of a goddess.

I was so enthralled that I sat staring, completely forgetting the camera in my lap. Scotch grabbed it and put it in my hands, to make sure I didn't forget to capture the moment.

The lions decided it was time to return to the business of gorging themselves and took a leisurely stroll right past our vehicle to get back to the carcass. There was some nuzzling, yawning and stretching before they hunkered down to resume feeding. The males were so full now that there was no argument about pecking order, and they even allowed the females to join in. The group surrounded the buffalo and the sound of teeth crushing bone filled the air, joining the smell of blood.

A year ago I would've been repulsed by this, but now I was completely fascinated. It occurred to me that I had indeed come a long way in my transition from North American City Dweller to South African Bush Woman.

"I know they aren't albinos; it's a recessive gene, right?" I asked Scotch.

"That's right. And the reason they're so rare is that both parents have to have that recessive gene. What makes it really strange is that two tawny lions can produce a white baby. If both have the recessive gene, out comes a white cub. Isn't that incredible?"

Pretty much everything I experienced at Tanda Tula was incredible, and I knew how lucky I was. I never took these opportunities for granted. After all, how many people ever actually get to see white lions, or become acquainted with the curious behaviour of a resident rhino?

It was Foremen who introduced me to the old rhino known as Mithenge-thenge. We were driving toward what seemed to me to be a very unremarkable spindly knobthorn tree. The only thing I could see that was unusual was the large grey boulder underneath it. I would have gone right past, but Foremen pulled over. Only then did I see that it wasn't a boulder, it was a rhino!

Foremen explained that to this particular rhino, that small tree was very special indeed.

"He's an old guy, that rhino. We don't know exactly how old, but you can see that the pads of his rear legs are worn down from marking his territory. He does that by dragging his dung-covered feet.

"His territory is huge – it takes him close to two weeks to mark and patrol it. And once that big job is done and he gets back, we always find him sleeping in this exact same spot, under this little knobthorn on the bare ground. The tree doesn't provide food or shade, but it obviously provides some kind of comfort to the rhino."

"Is that typical rhino behaviour?" I asked. "Do they tend to have a favourite spot?"

"No, it's not typical at all. I can't explain it, but it's really interesting. We see him with other rhinos in other places, so we know he's still social and mating, but he always comes back to this particular spot alone. We now call it the Mithenge-thenge tree."

Just then, the old boy stirred. I thought he was about to get up, but he just rearranged himself, extending his front legs forward and placing his chin on the ground between them, sprawling out like a cat in the sunshine. One eye opened, and then closed just as quickly. The ears remained on high alert, however, sweeping back and forth, listening for anything that might be worth getting up for. Apparently there was nothing worthwhile, so he went back to sleep.

We watched him dozing peacefully and I wondered how anyone could want to kill such a beautiful creature for the sake of his horn.

"I wonder what he dreams about?" I pondered aloud.

One of our guests at the back of the Land Rover was quick to supply the answer.

"When he's not here, I bet he dreams about this tree."

Probably the most uncommon sighting I experienced was of a mammal most people have never even heard of. The pangolin is a truly unique creature. The first time I saw a photo of one on the internet, I imagined that if an anteater mated with a pine cone, that's what the offspring would look like.

I'd first learned about these elusive armoured creatures in my textbook, *Smithers' Mammals of Southern Africa*. Unfortunately, they were very well known to the people of

China and Vietnam, where a serving of pangolin in a restaurant will cost about $250. Pangolin scales – which are made of keratin, much like rhino horn and our own fingernails – are sold at about $50,000 to $60,000 per kilogram, making them one of the most expensive illegal natural remedies on the market. These shy animals have the unhappy distinction of being the most trafficked mammal in the world.

Most of the guides who worked in the Timbavati Game Reserve had spent their entire lives living in the bush, and few of them had ever seen one of these solitary nocturnal creatures. When we heard over the radio that one had been spotted out in the open, everyone with a vehicle available jumped at the chance to see it.

As always, the comfort and safety of the animal came first, so only one vehicle at a time was allowed to make its way to where the pangolin had made its uncharacteristic daylight appearance. Normally, when they feel threatened, they curl up into a tight ball, but this guy had decided to show us his entire body, hiding only his face in a crevice between two rocks. He seemed to be operating on the theory that if he couldn't see us, we couldn't see him. Had we meant him any harm, his strategy would've been a disaster, but in the end all was well and we left with photos and a great story to tell.

While all these rare sightings were truly amazing, one of the most common and even most reviled animals in Africa was fast becoming one of my favourites. Hyenas really do get a bad rap. In movies they're portrayed as ugly, dirty, vile-smelling villains. They're accused of being opportunistic scavengers, when in fact they're also very successful hunters. They even have the dubious honour of being included in the "Ugly Five" – the group considered to be the ugliest animals in Africa. But at Tanda Tula, I was fortunate to see these misunderstood animals in a completely different light.

There were two dens situated not far from the camp, and we had the opportunity to get to know and love the animals in both the clans that occupied the territory. We saw the pups shortly after they were born. They emerged from the den looking like fluffy black puppy-dogs. Sticking close to Mom and the other adults, they were playful and full of fun.

As parents, hyenas are among the best in the animal kingdom – they're loving, nurturing and protective of their young. They're a highly social group, with all the adults playing a role in rearing the youngsters.

As the pups grew, their coats began to change. Gradually their black fur turned grey, starting at the tips of the ears and then the head. Spots started to appear at the neck and worked their way down the entire body. As they got older, the young ones became more independent, and they were left alone at the den while the adults went off in search of food.

The first few times we found them on their own, they were quite timid and would scamper back to the den and disappear down the hole when the game-drive vehicles pulled up. But soon they became habituated to the vehicles, and then they became downright curious. One day a particularly bold pup put his front paws up on the running board of the Landy, then sniffed the rubber of the tires before losing interest and resuming a wrestling match with his siblings.

When the adults returned from the day's hunt, there was a big, happy, vocal family reunion, with the adult hyenas sniffing and licking each other, then the youngsters throwing themselves on the adults, first for attention, then for milk and the regurgitated food they had eaten during their foray.

Really, Disney's *The Lion King* notwithstanding, what's not to love?

17

Timbavati Game Reserve

June 2013

As my knowledge and understanding of animal behaviour deepened, so did my respect and affection for my students and the other members of the Tanda Tula staff. The fact that I had lived and worked alongside them shifted the dynamic, and I'd started to get to know many of them well enough to begin asking questions about their lives and experiences.

Harry, like his brother Smiling, was a bartender at the lodge. I hadn't been able to coax Smiling to come to class, but Harry was an enthusiastic and eager student. He had a great ear for language, and was already quite fluent in eight of South Africa's eleven official languages, including English and Afrikaans.

He wanted to work on learning French as well as improving his English. He was a quick study, and soon had a good repertoire of basic French phrases to use with some of the European and Canadian guests.

He loved to read aloud in English and was particularly fond of folklore tales that explained things like how the ostrich got its long neck and why the warthog goes down on its knees when it eats.

I asked Harry about his life growing up and his previous education.

"I went to school until grade seven, but then my father passed away and I had to leave school to help support my family. I am number nine of fourteen kids. Like many men in our culture, my dad had three wives.

"In 1995 I got a job at Tanda Tula. My grandmother was afraid for me to come and work for white people. She thought they would beat me because I couldn't speak English and wasn't very educated.

"I started out as a gardener and one day I was clearing a path and I saw one of the guests coming. I was so scared I jumped into some bushes and hid, because I was afraid he would greet me and I wouldn't know how to answer.

"Eventually, I got braver, and with the help of the camp manager and many of the guests, I started to learn English. I was promoted to waiter, and then to bartender.

"My job changed my life. I never thought that I would meet people from all over the world and be able to speak to them in English. And now you and Anne are here to help us learn even more.

"I love your lessons; they open my mind to new possibilities. I take my schoolwork home and teach my children what I have learned.

"I am so grateful for this job. I am always learning new things and I can support my wife and three children, as well as my community in the village."

"Just one wife, Harry?" I prodded mischievously.

"Yes, one is enough for me," he laughed.

"And what does your grandmother think of all this now?" I asked.

Harry beamed his beautiful smile. "She loves it! And now she's not afraid of white people either. My brother and I have a charity called Kunavalela, which means 'raising hope'. She's very proud of our work. We do HIV/Aids counselling, we have a community garden to help with nutrition, and we also run a youth soccer programme to teach the kids teamwork and discipline.

"Now, many people of all races come out to the village to find out more about our projects and get involved. Grandmother really enjoys meeting everyone who comes out to see us. My job changed her life too."

Even though Smiling didn't come to class, I was gradually getting to know him better too. Some nights I'd act as one of the hosts at dinner, and would spend time with him in the bar as we prepared to welcome the guests back from the afternoon game drive.

One evening, the conversation turned to a subject I usually tried to avoid: religion. I was curious to find out how he reconciled the beliefs of his tribe with his Christian beliefs.

"When you pray, do you pray to your ancestors and the spirits, or do you pray to God?" I asked.

I was surprised to find out that Smiling didn't see a conflict between Christianity and the traditional beliefs.

"I pray to all of them," he said quite simply. "Really, what's the difference? If I pray to my ancestors, they are with God, so they can tell him. And if I pray to the spirits, they came from God, so they will tell him. But usually I just go direct. You know, cut out the middle man.

"That's why I don't bother much about ministers and priests. I don't need somebody telling me how to pray, when to pray and where to pray. I can do it anywhere, anytime and wherever I want to. And usually those guys are the ones doing all the things they tell you not to. I think there's some bad stuff going on with a lot of those guys."

Since we'd already tackled one taboo subject, I decided to push my luck and ask him about his politics.

"ANC, man! Always African National Congress. They gave us our freedom!" he proclaimed.

"True, Smiling," I agreed, "but it seems to me that the party is much changed since the glory days of Mr Mandela. There seems to be a lot of corruption, and I can't say that I'm too impressed with your president, Mr Zuma. All that foreign-aid money from Britain he spent on his house, or should I say palace? Come on, you know that's not right."

"It wasn't him. It was the people around him. He didn't know."

"I don't think that really builds your case for him. Are you saying he isn't even aware of what's going on in his own house? That he puts important decisions like how to spend foreign-aid dollars in the hands of other people and doesn't even ask how the money is being spent? That's just irresponsible. I really don't think he has the best interest of the people at heart. I know there'll never be another Mandela, but this guy seems to be the opposite. Besides, the cost of all his weddings and the wife and child support are enough to bankrupt the place. How many wives does he have, anyway?" I teased.

"Six wives and twenty children."

"That we know of."

"Yes, that we know of," he conceded with a laugh. "I know polygamy is not part of your culture, but it's still quite acceptable here."

I decided to leave the subject there.

Out on a drive once again with Scotch, I was introduced to a bit of his childhood. He had sized up his audience in the Land Rover, and decided that he'd find a taker or two among this adventurous group.

When we stopped for the evening ritual of sundowner drinks, he asked, "Who wants to play a game?"

"What kind of game?" asked a man who was honeymooning with his new bride.

"In Afrikaans, we call it *bokdrol spoeg*."

My Afrikaans is terrible, but I was pretty sure that *bokdrol* meant "buck droppings". I couldn't wait to see where this was going.

"What does that mean?" asked the honeymooner.

"Climb down and I'll show you," said Scotch with a sly grin.

The man clambered out the vehicle, and Scotch walked him over to a pile of antelope droppings.

"It's a spitting contest. Choose your weapon!" he exclaimed.

"You're kidding, right?"

"Nope. We start with antelope droppings, and eventually, when you get really good, you can use elephant droppings."

The guest stared at him in disbelief.

"Okay, I am kidding about the elephant droppings, but this is a game we played when I was growing up. While other kids played it with coffee beans or berries, if you grew up in the bush, you used impala or kudu droppings. The kudu droppings are a bit bigger if you like more weight."

Scotch picked up a couple of hard, dry pellets and weighed his options, literally. What criteria he used to choose his projectile remains a mystery. I'm no expert, but they looked about the same to me.

He drew a line in the sand with his foot to mark the starting line. He popped a pellet in his mouth, puffed out his cheeks and launched it. It arced through the air and landed several metres away.

Up next: the challenger. He paused for a moment, then quickly popped the poop into his mouth and spat ferociously. It shot out of his mouth in a straight line. Less arc meant more distance, and he easily bested his teacher.

While he won the contest, he lost the right to kiss his bride until after he'd brushed his teeth.

Time was flying by, and soon Johann and I would be celebrating our third wedding anniversary. I had no idea what I could get him until Scotch came to me with a business proposal.

"Want to buy some cows with me?" he asked out of the blue one day.

"Cows? You mean sides of beef? I don't have a freezer."

"No, real live cows. Umfazi, you really should have some. They are a great savings plan. You keep cows on your property and you sell the milk. Then, when you need to pay for something big, you sell them. When I need to pay my daughters' university fees, I sell some cows.

"I've heard about a guy who wants to sell six, and he's in a hurry so the price is good. What do you say? Three for you and three for me."

"Where on earth would I keep three cows? I mean that literally. I don't have any property," I pointed out.

"They can stay on my land," Scotch offered. "I will look after them with the rest of my herd, but you will have to come out and get to know them. It's very important that you know your cows."

What had sounded like such a bizarre idea just a few moments before suddenly seemed like an inspired plan. In some traditional cultures, cows were the currency used when negotiating lobola, the "bride price", which is property a prospective groom's head of family gives to the head of a prospective wife's family before a customary marriage. It would be a bit unusual, but why not give my groom three cows for our third anniversary?

248

"Yeah! Let's do it! Call the guy right away."

Scotch tried, but the cellphone signal was terrible. We even tried standing by the big leadwood tree which usually did the trick, but not this time. He couldn't get through.

The next day was the beginning of his two-week leave, so he'd go and see the seller in person when he got back to his village.

"Give me a call and let me know if we got them," I said.

I couldn't believe how excited I was getting about this, so it was a real disappointment when Scotch called me the next day with the news that the cattle had already been sold. He insisted that the dream wasn't dead, just delayed, and that he'd keep looking for a beef bargain that would get me into the cow business.

I was a bit deflated, knowing that any other anniversary gift I might come up with wouldn't be nearly as inspired. In the end, Johann received a bottle of red wine and an "I owe you" for three cows, which he still hopes to cash in.

18

Nyani Cultural Village, Hoedspruit, South Africa

July 2013

Foremen's mother was a sangoma, a traditional healer. He told me that this wasn't something she chose, but was a calling.

"Before you are born, your ancestors choose you, and call you to the profession. It is a very noble calling, one that is highly respected in our society. These people are more than healers of the physical. Yes, you can consult a sangoma for a headache or a stomach ailment, but they can also interpret your dreams, name your child, help with your relationship problems or guide you to choosing the right career."

"It sounds like a combination of doctor, psychiatrist, priest, psychic and witchdoctor," I observed.

"You are mostly right, but you must understand a sangoma is not a witchdoctor. While both use charms and muti [traditional medicines], a witchdoctor will use them to inflict harm on others. A sangoma uses his or her power, knowledge and skills only for good; their promise is to heal through love and compassion."

"How do they diagnose and heal?" I asked.

"They have a number of tools. To diagnose, they will throw the bones and read them. They will often hold something of yours or something that belongs to someone you love so that they can tune in to that vibration. They drum, chant, sing and dance. Once they have reached a diagnosis, you will get a prescription, which could be in the form of something you eat or drink, or they may recommend you perform some kind of purification ritual."

"Do you believe in all of this?" I asked.

"I do," he answered.

"So when you're ill, you would see your mother, not a doctor?"

"It depends on the severity. If I think I have malaria or something like that, I would see both. It doesn't have to be either or. And it's always better to be safe than sorry."

For days after my conversation with Foremen, I couldn't stop thinking about everything he'd told me about the role of the traditional healer in Shangaan culture. I found the whole thing utterly fascinating. It wasn't long before I'd decided to seek out a sangoma for a consultation myself.

There's a wonderful replica cultural village not far from where we live, where they try to keep traditional dancing and storytelling alive, and share the local tribal customs with visitors to South Africa. In the grounds of Nyani Village there's a traditional-healer's hut, and you can actually schedule an appointment with a real sangoma. After asking a few more questions of Foremen, I had an idea of what to expect, but it didn't quite prepare me for the reality.

I ducked down to enter the doorway of the rondavel, a small, dark, round hut. The sangoma was waiting inside. Her hair was a mass of braids, half of which hung over her face like a curtain. She invited me to sit on the blanket on the ground in front of her. She spoke little English, and I hoped that I'd be able to understand any message she had to give me.

She asked me for my wedding ring, held it in her hands for a few moments, then slid it under the mat in front of her. She rattled a can full of small bones, and cast them on the mat. Waving what looked like a cross between a broom and a magic wand over the bones, she began to chant loudly while rocking back and forth. I assumed this was how she summoned my ancestors and I wondered what all those Catholic French-Canadian spirits would make of this.

When she was done, she seemed to be in a trancelike state. She peered through her braids and asked, "What would you like to know?"

"Anything you can tell me," I responded, deciding not to try to control the experience.

She studied the bones for a few minutes, then said, "It's not your health. You are well. Marriage is mostly good. Money is a problem."

I couldn't argue with any of that.

"Can you tell me anything about our future?"

"You are going to go into business with another man and a woman. It has something to do with food. It will go well.

"Your husband loves you very much, but he has trouble talking. You must help him. He is not happy in his work."

She was spot-on about Johann and his work, but a business with another couple? I guessed time would tell.

"How can I help my husband?" I asked.

There was more chanting and rocking before she responded. She turned around and selected a glass jar from among the lotions and potions that lined the shelves behind her. Removing the lid, she selected two small twigs and handed them to me.

"One for you, one for him. Get a small glass of brandy. You must each chew on a stick, then each take a sip, then pour the rest of the brandy on to the ground as an offering to the ancestors. Then you will talk together better."

I sensed the appointment was coming to an end, so I just had to ask.

"Are you speaking to my ancestors? Can you tell me who is there? I was wondering if my great-uncle Ernest was part of the conversation."

She was quiet for a moment, trying to sense his presence. "He is here," she said at last. "They are all here – all those who came before you. They are enjoying the experience of your journey very much. They now see the world through your eyes. Know that they are always with you and that you must learn to feel for them. If you do, they will show themselves to you in many ways. When things happen, you will know it is them speaking to you.

"And you must understand that it is not just those you come from directly. Yes, your family is here, but I am also talking to the spirits of the earth, the stars and the animals. They are all interested because they are all part of you. They are experiencing life through you."

This struck me profoundly because it was a message that had been coming to me repeatedly through many sources. It was the core of all the spiritual books I'd been reading. It was coming through in my fledgling yoga and meditation practice. It was the basis of many conversations I was having with new people I was meeting.

At the most important level, the energy level, we're all connected; we are one. The energy of those who came before us didn't die and fade away. We all exist together in the Eternal

Moment of Now. I felt elated at the thought that the whole of the universe was on my side.

On my way home I stopped at the liquor store and bought a small bottle of brandy. When I got home, I put the twigs and the brandy on the table.

"What's this?" Johann asked, as he eyed the items suspiciously. If there's one thing my husband doesn't like to drink, it's brandy.

"Sorry, I know it's not to your taste, love, but I need you to humour me. It's our prescription from the sangoma. You only have to have a little sip. And you might be glad to have it because I have no idea what these twigs are going to taste like."

I explained what we were to do. Johann took it all in stride. He picked up a twig and popped it into his mouth.

"A bit bitter, but not too bad," he decided.

I chewed on mine as well, then took a little swig of brandy and offered the bottle to him. He gave an exaggerated grimace and took the prescribed sip. We went outside and finished the ritual by pouring the rest on to the grass.

"I hope the ancestors enjoyed that more than I did," Johann said.

"Well, that was supposed to help us talk, so let's see if it worked. I know you're finding it difficult at work, but you really don't say much. Please tell me what you're thinking."

"I don't talk about it because it's a good pay-cheque and we need it. Complaining won't solve anything, anyway. But it is a difficult place to be. According to the contract, English is supposed to be the language of the workplace, but hardly anybody speaks it. They all speak Portuguese, and I'm trying to learn, but I really don't understand much yet. It's isolating, and I really don't feel like I get much respect. It's fine if someone wants a tablet for a headache or something like that, but when I try to talk to them about health-and-safety issues, they really don't care.

"It's like I'm there because legally there has to be someone in the position, but they don't take it seriously. I've had this training, but I don't get to use it, and it's pretty frustrating. I'd like to quit, but we need the money and I can't seem to find anything else that pays as well that wouldn't mean us being apart even more than we are already. Remember what it was like when I was in Sudan? I worked three months at a stretch and was home for less than two weeks in between rotations."

"I wish you could quit too," I said. "Maybe the solution is coming and we just don't know it yet. The sangoma said we're going to go into business with another couple, something to do with food, and that it will be very successful."

256

"And you believe that?" he asked, a big grin spreading across his face. "You seem to have an awful lot of faith in this sangoma."

"Well, why shouldn't I? She said the twigs and the brandy would help you talk, and look at everything you've just told me."

"I don't know if it was because of the twigs and the brandy."

"Well, it was, even if only indirectly. My visit to the sangoma got us to have a good conversation about something that's been eating away at you. That's good enough for me. Now all we have to do is believe some new opportunity is on its way, and wait for it to present itself."

"I'll drink to that, if we can find something in the house that tastes better than that awful cheap brandy."

"You're in luck. I think there's still a bit of awful cheap wine in the box."

Epilogue

Oh my God, I live in Africa!

More often than not, that is still my first thought when I wake up in the morning. Even though we've been here in Hoedspruit for nearly two years now, I'm still amazed that life has brought me here.

And this is where I want to stay.

I live in Africa!

And to think it all started with the gift of an elephant.

I believe that small carving from my great-uncle Ernest played a big part in setting the course of my life's journey. I never forgot that gift or the extraordinary man who gave it to me. His example shaped my goals and dreams, and influenced my life in so many ways.

While I never made a conscious decision to create a collection, the elephants just kept coming. With each birthday, Christmas or other gift-giving occasion, the herd expanded. Eventually there were elephants galore in my house, peering down from the bookshelves, on the kitchen windowsill, on my desk, my bedside tables, even in the bathroom on the lip of the tub and perched on the back of the toilet. They were of all shapes and sizes. They were made of wood, glass and even crystal. There were elephants everywhere, and they made me happy.

I gave those elephants meaning. They came to represent joy, purpose, love, passion and giving.

As the years passed and the elephants continued to arrive, so did many opportunities. Many were everyday and ordinary but some, like the path that led me to Africa, were quite extraordinary. Even the events I'd labelled "bad" – in fact, especially those – have pushed my boundaries and helped me take another step toward becoming the person I want to be.

I am a work in progress, and I rejoice in the knowledge that I always will be. Life continues to bring me more to explore, and I'll continue to grow and change with each new experience.

Now I live in Africa, where the real elephants are – where the possibility exists that I can encounter one elephant or a whole herd of them on any given day. Each time I see one, I am filled with joy and I always stop to savour the privilege of being in its presence, because you never know when next you will receive the gift of an elephant.

When people ask Johann and me about our future plans, we can honestly tell them that we just don't know.

The opportunity we thought might come in Canada through the couple I'd met at the Safari Club didn't materialize because the man's contact had sold his business and moved on to other things. Is this a sign we're meant to stay in Africa?

Maybe. We know we want to stay here, but exactly how that will play out remains a mystery.

We're building a life here. Last time Johann came home from Mozambique, he did so in a new black Land Rover Freelander. When I say new, I mean new to us – it's a 1999 model he found on the internet. We'd been looking for an affordable bushworthy vehicle for the whole month he was home, and he even headed back to Johannesburg a day early to patrol the used-car lots there. He had no luck.

As soon as he got back to Moz, he went online to a used-car site, and just at that moment someone posted a vehicle that was exactly what we were looking for – and it was at a bargain price. Johann was the first to see the ad and he responded right away. He explained that he was in Mozambique and wouldn't be home for a month, but that he definitely wanted the vehicle and he would pick it up as soon as he landed in Johannesburg 28 days later. It was a complete leap of faith for both parties involved. Johann was buying the Landy sight unseen, and the seller had no idea who he was or if he was good for the money.

When Johann went to claim the car, the man told him that after he'd accepted Johann's offer, many others had called and emailed, some even offering him more than the asking price to try to entice him to break his promise. "I don't know why," he told Johann when they finally met, "but for some reason I knew it was supposed to be yours, so I turned down the cash and kept my word."

Johann loves Rover (as the Landy is now known) more than any other vehicle he has ever owned.

My trip to the sangoma at Nyani Village also produced an unexpected opportunity for me. As I was leaving my session, I ran into the woman who is the creative force behind the village. Maureen had recruited talented youth from the area, and over a period of years had turned them into a brilliant performance group called Roots of Rhythm.

I had met Maureen before, when the group had performed for the guests at Tanda Tula, and I was immediately attracted to her energy and dynamic personality. I knew she was someone I wanted to get to know better.

In speaking with her that day, I found a volunteer role for myself. I'm now applying my media background and experience to help promote Nyani Cultural Village, and I've had fun using my research and writing skills to create a script for the performers that explains some of the Shangaan tribal customs and traditions. It's a beautiful project that celebrates the local culture and allows talented youth to make a living doing what they love. I'm so happy to be a part of it.

The time is coming soon for us to take the next step, which will be daunting. Johann will quit his job in Mozambique. I'm building a strong social network here and Hoedspruit really is starting to feel like home for me but it's different for my husband. He's away so much that when he comes back, he sometimes feels like he's just visiting. It's now time for him to lay down some roots and build some friendships, after having spent so many years working in far-off and desolate places. We need to look for opportunities that will allow us to be together, in one place, all the time.

While it's a scary prospect to let go of what little security we have, we have faith that it will all fall together. And as the future unfolds, we'll do our best to enjoy each step on the path along the way.

I've completely given up on the notion of planning. Of the many, many changes in my life, this must surely be the biggest change of all. I used to feel the need to try to control everything. I organized and planned incessantly. As Mark Twain so famously observed, "I've lived through a thousand tragedies, none of which actually happened." I'm trying to keep that to a minimum by learning to relax, to stay open and to let life unfold as it will.

Since I've been living in Africa, I'm seeing the world differently. It feels like I'm waking up to how life actually works. I understand that what you put your focus on increases your experience, so I try to keep my attention on all the things that bring me joy and not dwell on things that don't. Often circumstances are beyond my control, but I can always change the way I choose to look at something. I realize now that the only thing I ever have to change is my mind.

Does that make it easy? Of course not. There are still many days when I lapse back into my old ways of thinking and my self-defeating habits.

But I am getting better at catching myself before I go too far down those old well-worn roads. And when I do find myself worrying or trying to control everything, I know that I need to get out of my own way.

I am learning to trust life, and as clichéd as it may sound, to go with the flow.

This is a process, and of course fear and anxiety still creep in and threaten to take over. In those moments, I acknowledge the feelings and try to move through them quickly and with as much grace as I can muster.

Most days I do see my life as the remarkable adventure that it is. I could never have planned any of this, but with the benefit of hindsight, I can see how events unfolded to create the path that brought me to where I stand today.

So here I am. For now? Forever? It really doesn't matter. Uncertainty can be frightening, but when not clouded by fear, it is truly liberating and can be seen as a great gift.

I try not to be attached to any particular outcome, secure in the knowledge that there will be a gift in anything that happens, even if it is not immediately apparent. While I am here in Africa I'm learning to live fully and presently in the moment, and I am experiencing more peace and joy than I ever could have imagined.

I am always grateful for the man who is my companion on this incredible journey.

Despite all the obstacles and challenges we've faced, and the uncertainty of what lies ahead, I can say without hesitation that I choose Johann again today.

Each day, we continue to create our happily-ever-after, moment by moment.

Ours is an amazing life, full of love and elephants.

About the author

In her native Canada, Jacquie Gauthier was a local radio and television personality, a playwright and producer, and for a short time, a politician. Her play *Jazzabel*, along with *Portraits*, the festival of one-woman shows she co-produced, was featured in Oprah Winfrey's *O* magazine.

Now, Jacquie is a certified nature guide, a teacher of English and adult literacy, a blogger and photographer, and – get this – a passionfruit farmer in South Africa, where she's busy creating her happily-ever-after with her beloved husband Johann. Their story was featured on an episode of the American television show *House Hunters International*.

Jacquie is the co-founder of and image co-creator at Two Girls and an Elephant, a company combining photography, art and elephant conservation. Visit the website at www.twogirlsandanelephant.com.

Jacquie hopes to have Sandra Bullock play her in the film adaptation of her first book.

Help Secure a Future for Elephants

The statistics are staggering; 36,000 African elephants are brutally slain by poachers every year. That's 96 a day. One elephant killed every 15 minutes. If the killing continues at this rate, there will be no elephants left in the wild in 2025. This is the deciding decade— a critical time in the life of this majestic, ecologically important animal.

The Elephant is what is known as a keystone species. Their activity influences the landscape, the plants and the other animals around them. When they knock down a tree, other animals gain access to the leaves for food and a new place to build a nest and breed. There is no better propagator of plant life. Their droppings deliver seeds to new locations, conveniently encased in fertilizer. Their impressive footprints catch rain water creating small pools for other animals to drink from. Virtually every move they make creates ripples through the ecosystem. The landscape of the African Bush will be forever changed without their majestic presence.

There are many organizations working to ensure the survival of elephants. Let's throw our support behind them to ensure the survival of this magnificent species.

Please visit our website and show your support

TWO GIRLS
and an
ELEPHANT

Photography, Painter and Papermaker

"Photography meets fine art and elephant conservation"

My friend Alicia Fordyce and I created *Two Girls and an Elephant*
to help support this important cause.

The concept of using elephant dung paper as the base for our art appealed
to us both. We love its organic look and feel, and view it as the ultimate in
recycling, creating something beautiful out of pure waste. Its use also
provides an opportunity to publicize the plight of the elephant in order to
raise funds and awareness for conservation.

Choose from our original paintings, prints, drawings and photographs,
or commission a unique work of art!

Originals and Prints come with a Certificate of Authenticity.
When you buy one of our prints, you take home an authentic piece
of Africa and you also support elephant conservation.
We donate a percentage of every sale to *Elephants Alive South Africa*.

Your support will make a difference!
Jacquie Gauthier

twogirlsandan**elephant**.com

Made in the USA
Middletown, DE
04 February 2024

48942753R00156